What Good Is Journalism?

What Good Is Journalism?

How Reporters and Editors
Are Saving America's Way of Life

Edited with an Introduction by
George Kennedy and Daryl Moen

University of Missouri Press
Columbia and London

Copyright © 2007 by
The Curators of the University of Missouri
University of Missouri Press, Columbia, Missouri 65201
Printed and bound in the United States of America
All rights reserved
5 4 3 2 1   11 10 09 08 07

Cataloging-in-Publication Data available from the
Library of Congress
ISBN 978-0-8262-1730-1 (hard cover : alk. paper)
ISBN 978-0-8262-1731-8 (pbk. : alk. paper)

♾™ This paper meets the requirements of the
American National Standard for Permanence of Paper
for Printed Library Materials, Z39.48, 1984.

Designer: Stephanie Foley
Typesetter: The Composing Room of Michigan, Inc.
Printer and binder: The Maple-Vail Book Manufacturing Group
Typefaces: Garamond 3 and American Typewriter Condensed

The University of Missouri Press acknowledges the generous
contribution of the Missouri School of Journalism, Office of the
Dean toward the publication of this book.

Contents

What Good Is Journalism?

Introduction

This is not a book of criticism. Neither the practitioners nor the consumers of American journalism suffer from any lack of criticism. This is, instead, a book of explanation. Its purpose is to show readers the most important roles that journalism, with all its well-documented faults, plays in the world's oldest democracy. Those roles, we argue, are vital to the health of the democracy.

Journalism tells us most of what we know about the world beyond our own experience. Journalism goes where its audience cannot or will not. Journalism keeps daily watch on the actions of government and the other powerful institutions of society. Journalism exposes wrongdoing and injustice. Journalism explains in everyday language the findings of science and the arguments of philosophy. Journalism pulls together and organizes obscure but important facts to create useful knowledge. Journalism tells stories of heartbreak and heroism, of triumph and disaster, of the endless fascinations in ordinary life. Journalism is the glue of information that holds a complex nation together.

We are not, of course, the first to note the symbiotic relationship between journalism and democracy. The nation's founders understood it well, and so they included freedom of the press among the essential liberties protected by the First Amendment to the U.S. Constitution.

James Madison, the principal author of the First Amendment, wrote in 1822, "A popular government without popular information or the means of acquiring it is but a prologue to a farce or a tragedy, or perhaps both."

Thomas Jefferson had written, even more famously, in 1787, "The basis of our government being the opinion of the people, the very first object

1

should be to keep that right; and were it left to me to decide whether we should have a government without newspapers, or newspapers without a government, I should not hesitate a moment to prefer the latter." Less often quoted is Jefferson's qualifier: "But I should mean that every man should receive those papers, and be capable of reading them."

The Founders were also among the first journalism critics. As president, Jefferson was subjected to the attacks of the viciously partisan press of that era. He responded, as public figures have ever since, "Nothing can now be believed which is seen in a newspaper. . . . I will add that the man who never looks into a newspaper is better informed than he who reads them; inasmuch as he who knows nothing is nearer to truth than he whose mind is filled with falsehoods and errors." He proceeded to suggest, "Perhaps an editor might begin a reformation in some such way as this: Divide his paper into 4 chapters, heading the 1st, Truths. 2d, Probabilities. 3d, Possibilities. 4th, Lies. The first chapter would be very short . . . ."

In the two centuries since Madison and Jefferson wrote, American journalism has generated criticism from across the political spectrum and from both within and without its own ranks. What was probably the first book-length critique was published in 1859 by a disgruntled former editor. Lambert Wilmer's title revealed his perspective: *Our Press Gang; or, a Complete Exposition of the Corruptions and Crimes of the American Newspapers.* Present-day critics are equally pungent. From the right, Bernard Goldberg has published one book titled *Bias* and a follow-up called *Arrogance.* From the left, Eric Alterman's title asked rhetorically *What Liberal Media?* James Fallows's less-ideological attack is *Breaking the News.*

If criticism is nothing new, another development seems to be. That is the sharp decline in the levels of respect and trust granted by the public to journalism. Just to take one measure, the percentage of respondents to the Gallup Poll who rated journalists' ethics high or very high declined from 33 percent in 1976 to 21 percent in 2004. In another measure of the low esteem in which Americans hold their journalism, a national survey by the Pew Research Center for the People and the Press showed in 2003 that 59 percent of respondents thought news organizations are politically biased, only 35 percent thought news organizations usually get their facts straight, and 55 percent thought they don't care about the people they report on.

With declining trust and multiplying sources of information, mainly on the Internet, have come declining audiences. In 2004, when Gallup asked in a national survey where Americans get their news, just 51 percent said they watch local television news every day, only 44 percent said they read a local newspaper every day, and a mere 36 percent said they watch network news every day. All those numbers have declined by more than 20 percentage points in a quarter century. Network television news, in fact, has lost 44 percent of its audience since 1980. The Gallup survey shows that in just the last two years, network news lost 7 percent of its audience and local television news 6 percent. Newspapers showed no statistically significant loss. Only news on the Internet showed a gain, from 15 to 20 percent who said they use it daily. While the Internet is clearly stealing its audience from the traditional media, these surveys and other studies show just as clearly a declining appetite for news, especially among young adults.

It is possible we will look back at the beginning of this millennium as a transition period from the dominance of print and broadcast media to digital media. As broadband reaches more homes, more readers are turning away from the printed newspaper and network television to the Web. Many of them are going to newspaper Web sites, especially for local news. That's good news for newspapers, which will try to sell a combined print and digital audience to advertisers. However, before the day arrives when Web advertising can begin to support sizable news staffs, newspapers will struggle to adjust their economic model. Some fear that newspapers, which provide the bulk of the news you read on such meta news sites as Google, Yahoo, and AOL, may disappear or become minor players in the national conversation. The same concern applies to the other "traditional" news media. All this is obviously bad news for journalists and the companies that employ them, but why should anybody else care?

Because, as Madison and Jefferson understood, a self-governing people must be a well-informed people. A healthy democracy requires healthy journalism. Thomas Patterson, a political scientist at Harvard who has studied both journalism and politics, argues that unreasonably negative journalism drives down interest in politics and government. He reports that his research also shows that "Interest in news and interest in politics are inextricably linked. . . . The news is a window onto the world of public affairs."

Patterson's point, and that of the Founders, is where this book begins. The authors, all faculty members at the University of Missouri School of Journalism (and all critics, to varying degrees, of the journalism we teach and study), hope to show by the real stories of real people two things: First, that American journalism, taken as a whole, is better than its critics admit; and second, that good journalism is a force for good in the lives of individuals and the nation.

We begin by reporting on the first national survey to examine how Americans use journalism and why they value it. Then we trace the history of American journalism through the struggles and legal rulings that have increased freedom and access to information, not just for journalists but for all Americans. Then come real stories of journalism's value, including the story of NPR, the one national news source that is actually adding audience by providing listeners not only the news but also a continuing connection to the life of the nation. There's also the story of the *Anniston Star,* a small daily newspaper in Alabama that has been for more than a century the center and the conscience of its community. And there are the important stories told by journalists using the traditional tools of investigative reporting and the revolutionary new techniques of computer-assisted reporting. In both cases, citizens are served by the watchdogs of journalism. Another chapter tells the stories of the unknown heroes of newly free nations and newly independent journalism.

Last but not least, we offer some suggestions to the consumers of journalism—suggestions for making sure you get the news you need and the commentary you want.

In that spirit, please consider this an invitation to join in one of the most important conversations free people can have. That is the conversation we're hoping to further with this book, the conversation about journalism and democracy.

Americans and Journalism
We Value but Criticize It

Look past the ideologues and professional critics, and you'll find that the relationship between Americans and journalism is a complicated mix of appreciation and anger, dependence and distrust. The results of a unique national survey show that citizens want and need the work of journalists—but that journalists must do a better job of living up to and explaining their own ideals. In succeeding chapters, you will see how those ideals have strengthened and continue to serve democracies here and abroad. One coauthor of this chapter, George Kennedy, is a professor emeritus at the Missouri School of Journalism. The other, Glen Cameron, holds the Maxine Gregory chair at the school.

Donald Rhymer, David Hudson, and Donna Hicks are critical consumers of American journalism. They see evidence of bias. They don't like invasions of privacy. They think there's too much reporting of the negative and not enough of the positive. They suspect journalists are too easily influenced by powerful individuals and institutions.

They also think journalism is mainly a force for good. They find it helpful in understanding what's going on and in thinking about public issues. They agree that journalists should press for access to information government would like to conceal. They strongly believe that freedom of the press is important to our system of government. In general, they trust what they read and hear. Overall, the grade they would give to American journalism is "good."

Mr. Rhymer, forty-five, is a truck driver in New Jersey. Mr. Hudson, forty-seven, manages a computer network in Alabama. Ms. Hicks, sixty-seven, works in local government in Colorado. Mr. Rhymer and Mr. Hud-

5

son both describe themselves as conservative, Ms. Hicks as middle-of-the road. Mr. Rhymer is African-American; Mr. Hudson and Ms. Hicks are white.

What the three have in common is a complicated set of beliefs about the shortcomings, the contributions, and the importance of journalism in America. A national survey undertaken for this book shows that those beliefs are widely shared by people across the country. We Americans, it seems, are clear-eyed about our journalism. We see and object to its flaws while we understand and appreciate its importance. We use it and need it. We just wish journalists did a better job.

This examination of journalism comes at a time when both the nature of news and the ways in which it is transmitted are changing. Newspaper and television journalists tell us most of what we know about our local communities, about our nation, and about the world. But these mainstream media are shedding workers to cut costs as more and more consumers are turning to new sources of news on the Internet.

The traditional sources of news are also undergoing a continuing barrage of criticism, especially from the political right, that has contributed to a decline in credibility and something approaching a crisis of confidence among journalists.

This study was undertaken to try to get a better understanding of the relationship between Americans and journalism.*

While three-quarters of respondents think the news is overly negative, three-quarters also think journalism helps us understand what's going on in America. While more than eight out of ten see bias in news coverage, more than nine out of ten believe that freedom of the press is important to our system of government. While nearly two-thirds say journalists often invade people's privacy, more than eight out of ten agree that it is important for journalists to press for access to information about government, even when officials want to keep it quiet.

This intriguing mix of criticism and support comes through strongly in

---

*A note on methods: Our survey was conducted by the Center for Advanced Social Research at the University of Missouri. Respondents, 495 of them, were chosen at random to be representative of the adult U.S. population as a whole. They were contacted by telephone in the spring and summer of 2004 and asked more than fifty questions about their perceptions of and experience with journalism. Respondents were asked whether they would be willing to answer follow-up questions. One of the authors of this chapter then reinterviewed some of them by telephone, including Ms. Hicks, Mr. Hudson, and Mr. Rhymer, whose answers to the survey appeared typical. These two steps produced the statistics and the comments you see here.

the study. The responses showed the same complaints revealed in other surveys. This poll, however, asked some questions others have not. In addition to asking about general attitudes, this survey asked about the roles journalism plays in people's lives, and in the life of the nation. It asked respondents to weigh the importance of journalism to them and to the democracy. It gave them a chance to assess both credibility and overall importance. The findings are at once cautionary and hopeful.

The findings are also important, because—as the overwhelming majority of respondents agreed—journalism is important to the daily lives of citizens and to the health of the democracy itself. That's a fundamental point that journalism's critics, and journalists themselves, too often overlook.

Mr. Hudson could be speaking for most in the survey when he concluded, "Journalism may be slanted, but it's the best way to get the news. If you take away journalism, you'd want it back with whatever flaws it has."

The flaws he sees are also seen by most of his fellow citizens.

The survey asked, "How often do you see social or political bias in news coverage?" Mr. Hudson answered "somewhat often." Of all the respondents, 85 percent said they see bias "somewhat often" or "very often." Only 13 percent said "rarely" or "never." Almost half said the bias they see is "liberal"; about one-third said it is "conservative."

The bias Mr. Hudson sees "is a little more weighted toward the left," he said. "Some do try to be fair," he added. What he really resents is that "some journalists are slanted but won't own up to it." He applauds Rush Limbaugh and other commentators of the right and left for being open about their leanings.

Ms. Hicks, who sees bias "very often," sees it a bit differently. She sees journalists of both liberal and conservative bent, but she worries more about what Americans aren't being told, about foreign wars and domestic issues. "There's a good deal of censorship. Some significant information is being buried. We get snapshots." She concedes, "I don't know whether journalists are being stonewalled or maybe the stories just don't sell. . . . Maybe I'm in a minority."

Maybe she is. A survey by the Pew Research Center for the People and the Press, done in 2002, found many Americans critical of the degree of patriotism of the press. In November 2001, asked whether the "news media stands up for America," 69 percent agreed. Six months later, that number had fallen to 49 percent. The burst of patriotic emotion that affected journalists and audiences immediately after 9/11 faded quickly.

One of those critics is Donald Rhymer, a self-described "Army brat" who grew up paying attention to the news at the insistence of his father, a career soldier. Mr. Rhymer thinks journalists are too often unfair to the military. "Even with war, when that Marine shot that Iraqi—that's what happened, but as a U.S. citizen there's no way I'd have brought that back to this country." In his view, "Not all reporting is objective." Like 70 percent of those surveyed, he wishes reporters would just stick to the facts. "I don't want the media interpreting for me."

The media bias he sees is definitely liberal. "If I listen to the liberal media, George Bush is a bumbling fool. That's insulting to the American people. If I'm going to show Bush's weaknesses, show his strengths, too." Mr. Rhymer says he tries to be objective, even about journalism. "It's an industry, and you're trying to make money, so you do stories people like." His objectivity leads him to the overall assessment that "compared to other countries, it's as good as it gets."

(Later in this chapter, we address the biases of American journalism, which we argue have little to do with politics and a great deal to do with the role journalism plays in a free society. Our survey did not attempt to measure the effect on Mr. Rhymer and others of the drumbeat of ideological criticism that has pounded the profession in recent years, mainly from pundits and politicians of the right. Our later discussion may explain the causes of that criticism, if not its effects.)

Most of our respondents share Mr. Rhymer's understanding that journalism in this country is also a business. Ms. Hicks's concern about pressures from above is also widely shared. That shows in the responses to this question: "In general, do you think the news media are pretty independent, or are they often influenced by powerful people and organizations?" By a margin of more than three to one, the response was "often influenced."

Among the skeptics is Kathy Woods, a fifty-seven-year-old house cleaner who lives in a small town in Tennessee. "People who have the money control the newspapers, the TV. . . . They're the ones who get reported on. The little guy may need help, but their stories don't get told." One of the most influential forces, she said, is the government. Like Ms. Hicks, she suspects that the public isn't getting "the exact truth" about sensitive issues. She thinks it is very important for journalists to dig for information, even when officials want to keep it hidden.

Ms. Woods is also among the two-thirds of respondents who said journalists "often invade people's privacy." She said, with anger in her voice, "They push into people's private lives. They go too far. That's not right." She blames television, especially. That's one reason, she said, that she and her husband prefer to read the newspaper and *Time* magazine. "They're not quite so sensational. TV is more drama."

Most of our respondents rely on more than one medium for their news. Many, like Ms. Woods, see keeping informed as a duty of a good citizen. Three-quarters said they usually watch the local television news at least three days a week. Two-thirds said they read their local newspaper at least three days a week.

But do people believe what they read and hear? Many studies have suggested that the public's trust in what journalists report has declined in recent years. For example, in 1998 the American Society of Newspaper Editors launched a major effort to improve credibility with a study that showed 73 percent in a national survey agreeing with the statement "I have to admit that lately I've become more skeptical about the accuracy of anything I hear or read in the news." A Gallup poll in 2004 showed that television news and newspapers ranked near the bottom, just above big business and far below the military, the police, and organized religion, when Americans were asked how much confidence they have in major institutions.

Our respondents, too, have their doubts. For Kimberly Huggins, credibility "depends on what the story is about." David Hudson questions many journalists' methods. "I don't know what journalists are taught, but so many times they gather a few facts and throw a story together without talking to enough people." For Mike McCormick, "You have to take it with a grain of salt."

Overall, though, our survey found substantial levels of belief. The statement: "In general, American journalism is credible." The response: 62 percent agreed; 19 percent disagreed. By margins of more than two to one, respondents said they trust the information in their local newspapers and broadcast stations.

Mr. McCormick, who supervises medical records in Oklahoma, keeps up with newspapers and television, and listens to sports talk shows for entertainment. Does he consider himself well informed? "As much as I want to be," he replied. The news, he said, "is very important to me." At fifty-eight, he worries that his younger coworkers don't share that sense of importance. "They don't read the papers or watch the news. That's a scary situation," he said. "A lot of young people have no clue what's going on. They don't seem to care."

A recent study by political scientist Thomas Patterson of Harvard University suggests that Mr. McCormick may be correct. The Patterson study found that 42 percent of adults younger than thirty years of age expressed little or no interest in politics. That figure was almost twice as high as for the older generation. Similarly, about half the young adults said they pay little attention to the news. Patterson found a close relationship between caring about public affairs and paying attention to the news.

Kimberly Huggins, twenty-five, admits to being in that group. "My mom is more of a news person," she said. She herself is just too busy to devote much time to the news, she said. She works long hours in the candy store she recently opened with her mother in their small Georgia town. Still, she said, "My mom and I were talking about a story in the newspaper today." It was a story about an election recount, and she wondered why the journalist referred to those seeking the recount as "dissidents." Was that bias or just poor word choice, she questioned.

Even with her limited time for journalism, Ms. Huggins finds it useful. "It does help" in understanding the world around her, she said. "Even if I don't agree, I do understand the popular opinion. It's good to know what's going on."

That attitude, like the perceptions of bias and intrusiveness, is widely shared. Asked "how useful is journalism in your daily life," 58 percent of those surveyed found it useful, with only 15 percent saying it is not. In response to another question, 60 percent agreed that "I personally benefit from what journalists provide." Twenty-two percent disagreed. Coming at that point from another direction, the survey asked "how valuable" each of the main news media are. Ranking highest were television and newspaper journalism, each with two-thirds of respondents saying it is valuable. Radio journalism came next, with 56 percent. Then came magazine journalism, with 38 percent, and the Internet, with 36 percent.

Three-quarters of those surveyed agreed with Ms. Huggins that "Journalism helps me understand what is going on in America." The same percentage agreed that "Journalism helps me to be more thoughtful about public issues." In both cases, fewer than 15 percent disagreed.

Our survey also yielded mainly positive assessments of several of the traditional roles of journalism. By 65 percent to 18 percent, respondents agreed that "Journalists are good watchdogs over public officials." Some, including Donna Hicks, want the watchdogs to have sharper teeth. "I wish we had a watchdog press, a press that kept them honest," said this government worker.

By 53 to 28 percent, respondents agreed that journalists do a good job of protecting the public from abuses of power. Donald Rhymer, despite his view that journalists are too often unfairly negative toward the military, is one who wishes that protection were even stronger, and that journalists stirred up more outrage about abuses they uncover. Or, as he put it, "When it's time to scream, they don't scream."

How important the watchdog role is to the consumers of journalism is made clear by the overwhelming response to a related statement. The statement: "It is important for journalists to press for access to information about our government, even when officials would like to keep it quiet." The response: 83 percent agreed; only 8 percent disagreed.

Similarly, 81 percent agreed with the statement "It is important that journalists dig into data that is hard for ordinary citizens to understand." Just 11 percent disagreed.

The foundation of the relationship between the public and its journalism rests on a shared understanding of journalism's place in the democracy. Our survey suggests that the understanding is clear and the foundation strong. The statement: "The freedom of the press is important to our system of government." The response: 93 percent agreed; 4 percent disagreed. Even more striking than the overall response is that two-thirds of the respondents chose the strongest possible level of agreement.

When we asked whether people thought journalism in America has too little or too much of that freedom, 75 percent responded that there is either too little or about the right amount of freedom. Only 23 percent said the press is too free.

Responses to this survey provide considerable cause for optimism among all who value journalism. By comfortable majorities, the consumers of journalism told us that they value journalism and recognize its importance in their lives. The statistics and the follow-up interviews show broad support for press freedom and for the exercise of that freedom to question the powerful and protect the weak.

However, the majorities are just as big when those consumers came to identify journalism's flaws. Three-quarters of our respondents said the news media are "too negative." Eighty-five percent said they see social or political bias in news coverage, and by 48 to 30 percent they see that bias as liberal rather than conservative. Seventy percent said the news media are "often influenced" by the powerful. Nearly two-thirds said journalists often invade people's privacy.

This mix of results suggests that Americans think journalism is important, but that we wish journalists did a better job of living up to their own ideals of fairness, independence, and respect. That those are, in fact, core principles of American journalists was illustrated by the results of a study done in 2004 by the Pew Research Center for the People and the Press. Asked to identify the essentials of their craft, practicing journalists and news executives agreed that "accuracy and balance in reporting represent the essence of journalism," the study concluded. These journalists also agreed that their first obligation is to their audience and that the watchdog role is essential. They strongly supported the principle of independence.

How can we explain the gap between the aspirations of journalists and the perceptions of those who see their work? In recent years, that question has been tackled in scores of books, whose authors range from avowed partisans to scholars. Much of the most trenchant criticism has come from within the ranks of journalists themselves. For example, former television journalist Bernard Goldberg has written two books, one titled *Bias* and the other *Arrogance,* in which he imputes those failings to the elites of journalism, especially the television networks. From the other side, Eric Alterman, who holds a doctorate in history from Stanford and works as a journalist of the left, has written *What Liberal Media?* He argues that the forces of ownership and elite status incline most mainstream journalism toward conservatism. James Fallows, a writer of magazine articles and books, in *Breaking the News* decries the insularity and elitism of leading journalists, which he says results in both bias and arrogance.

The theme that runs through these books and many other critiques is the problem of bias. Psychologists have shown that bias, like beauty, resides at least partly in the eye—or the mind—of the beholder. However, if it were true that American journalism is guilty of consistent bias that distorts the views of the world it presents every day, the journalists' self-assigned principles of accuracy and balance would be undermined.

To a great degree, the problem of journalistic bias is peculiarly American. In much of the world, journalism—especially broadcast journalism—is controlled directly or indirectly by the government. Bias is required and generally assumed. In Europe, where print journalism is free of government controls and broadcast journalism largely so, the usual pattern is for the news media to be openly partisan or ideological. In Great Britain, for example, the major newspapers are clearly identified as leaning either left or right, while the publicly owned BBC is generally seen as not taking sides.

In this country, by contrast, the prevailing standard of mainstream journalism, print and broadcast, is something called objectivity. That has been true for roughly a century. Before that, as the introduction to this book recalled, journalists were frequently active partisans. At the risk of oversimplifying, it is fair to say that objectivity was adopted as a confluence of economic, technological, and political forces all pushed journalism in the direction of trying to reach the broadest possible audience. The partisan press generally reached only readers who shared the editors' views. If the press were objective, owners reasoned, they could gain a larger audience share and attract more advertising. Originally, objectivity was intended as the application to journalism of the scientific method. At the heart of that method were independence, reliance on factual evidence, and openness about method and results.

Those remain the bases of journalistic practice, though practitioners and scholars continue to argue about both the desirability and the attainability of true objectivity in an enterprise so intensely human as journalism. Some critics worry that more superficial standards, especially "balance," have replaced the original goal of scientific objectivity. Also, journalists typically are not as transparent about their methods as scientists are.

Still, the question recurs: In a practice committed to objectivity, how does bias creep in? Or does it?

One likely source of bias would be journalists themselves. Here's a quick composite portrait of the American journalist, drawn from a study called *The American Journalist in the 21st Century.* The 2002 study, funded by the Knight Foundation and conducted by scholars from Indiana University, consisted of a survey of more than one thousand practicing journalists. Its findings:

• The typical American journalist is a white male, forty-one years old, college-educated, and earning about $43,600 a year. The journalist places high value on the traditional principles of the craft, with heavy emphasis on the watchdog role and growing concern about such controversial practices as deception and invading privacy.

• About one-third of American journalists are women. Not quite one in ten is a person of color. Nearly 90 percent are college graduates, with about half having majored in journalism or communication. The number identifying themselves as Democrats has fallen by 7 percent in a decade, to 37 percent. The number of Republicans increased from 16 to 19 percent, and the number of independents is about 33 percent. There were about 116,000 journalists working in the mainstream media in 2002.

A reasonable generalization, then, would be that American journalists are middle-class, closing in on middle age, and politically middle of the road. Add to that the professional ethic of objectivity, the college and on-the-job indoctrination into that ethic, and the fact that the vast majority of mainstream journalists work for big, publicly owned corporations. The case for bias in the workforce is weak.

There is, however, bias built into the practice of journalism. The source is so obvious that most commentators overlook it. Its pervasiveness goes a long way toward explaining the widespread public perception of bias, especially liberal bias. Its nature can also explain why journalists themselves are so resistant to the accusation.

This built-in bias lies in the very job description of journalism—to remain apart from the power structure, to question and when necessary challenge authority, to expose injustice and wrong-doing, and to protect the powerless from the powerful. All these are roles that were applauded by healthy majorities in our survey. But all are roles much more likely, in America, to be identified as "liberal" rather than as "conservative."

The highest honors in journalism usually go to work that in some way challenges or questions the status quo. The folk heroes of a generation were the two young *Washington Post* reporters who questioned authority so persistently during the Watergate scandal of the early 1970s that their work helped to bring down a president.

So the societal role of journalism is to be critic rather than cheerleader, questioner rather than accepter of authority, watchdog rather than lapdog. The paradox is that the products of that role, that job description, are at once what society requires and what it criticizes. Journalists welcome the role but resent the criticism.

There is a countercurrent that produces in mainstream journalism an even more fundamental conservatism. That deeper current is fed by economics and tradition. Its result is that the challenging, the questioning, the reforming instincts of American journalists play out within the constraints of a relatively narrow political and ideological spectrum.

Compare American politics to the rest of the world and you will see that in this country both the left and right wings are effectively absent. We have no kings or dictators, no communists or socialists in public office or public discourse. Similarly, in mainstream American journalism there is little or no questioning of the two-party system or market capitalism. Nor is there much questioning of the society's prevailing myths, such as equality of opportunity or social mobility. In the world's oldest democracy, journalists, like the rest of society, take some structures, and some limits, for granted. In societies that are not free—such as America in 1776—a free press is an agent of revolution. In a society with freedoms so well established as in twenty-first-century America, freedom of the press is part of the status quo.

Just as a scientist studies every detail of an experiment but seldom thinks about the laboratory itself, so do the critics of journalism see its everyday products and think of them as liberal while seldom recognizing the fundamental conservatism of the status quo to which both critics and journalists belong. Journalists themselves are guilty, of course, of the same myopia.

The very definition of journalism also accounts, at least in large part, for the "negativity" to which most of our respondents—and majorities in other surveys—object. A dictionary defines "news" as "new developments . . . recent happenings." Even in the world of twenty-four-hour coverage and the infinite capacity of the Internet, not every new development or recent happening can be reported. Journalists define "news" as those recent happenings that are likely to affect the lives of their audiences, or that are likely to capture the interest of people already bombarded with information and harassed by demands on their time and their attention. Along with relevance, novelty and conflict are key elements in news as journalists, and most audience members, see it.

Smoothly functioning government, airplanes that arrive on time, businesspeople who obey the law, sunny days and calm seas—those may all be recent happenings, but few journalists and few consumers of journalism would define any of them as news. Journalists focus their efforts, and the public's attention, on the disruptions of everyday normalcy. Crime, corruption, war, disaster—those are news, along with such routine but relevant developments as city council meetings and Super Bowls.

While this structural explanation accounts for most of the negative tone of the nightly news and morning front pages, journalists can be faulted for their widespread failure to pay sufficient attention to what has been called "the journalism of hope." That is, or would be, reports of problems that include possible solutions, accounts of disasters that focus on recovery efforts, political reporting that emphasizes what candidates want to achieve as well as their shortcomings. We didn't ask in our survey whether that content would relieve the gloom most respondents see, but other studies have suggested that it would.

Journalists are too often also guilty of professional sins that can't be explained by their societal role or their training. One is invasion of privacy. In the interviews for this study, examples of journalistic intrusion into moments of grief or the turning of a spotlight onto the life of a private citizen brought anger to people's voices. Asked how journalists might improve their work, Kathy Woods of Tennessee responded instantly, "I would like to see them back off of people and give them some privacy." A retired banker from Minnesota, who didn't want her last name used, complained about excessive coverage of court cases: "They invade people's privacy at times when they shouldn't be around. That's what I object to."

Many journalists recognize the problem. The code of ethics of the Society of Professional Journalists, under the heading "Minimize harm," says that journalists should "show compassion for those who may be affected adversely by news coverage." It goes on to say that journalists should "recognize that private people have a greater right to control information about themselves than do public officials and others who seek power, influence or attention. Only an overriding public need can justify intrusion into anyone's privacy." The 65 percent of our respondents who said that journalists often invade privacy would agree.

In fact, a reasonable inference from our study and others is this: If journalists did a better job of sticking to their own principles, and a better job of explaining those principles to their audience, both press and public would be well served.

What makes that inference reasonable is the deeper reality that free journalism and free people are mutually dependent. Neither can exist for long without the other. Journalists have made that argument for generations. Coming from them, it can appear self-serving. The most important finding of this study is that the free people, the nonjournalists, see the relationship, too. The consumers of journalism, it turns out, have a more balanced, perhaps a more sophisticated, understanding than either the practitioners or the professional critics.

Kimberly Huggins, the young candy story owner in Georgia, put it this way: "There are a lot of outrageous things, but how do you curb the outrageous things without getting in the way of things we need to know? It's good to know what's going on."

Sources

The content of this chapter comes from an original survey conducted for this book, follow-up telephone interviews by the authors, and books and articles, either in print or online. Donna Hicks, David Hudson, Kimberly Huggins, Mike McCormick, Donald Rhymer, and Kathy Woods were all respondents to the original survey who agreed to be recontacted for additional questions.

Other Sources, In Print

Alterman, Eric. *What Liberal Media?* New York: Basic Books, 2003.

Fallows, James. *Breaking the News: How the Media Undermine American Democracy.* New York: Pantheon Books, 1996.

Goldberg, Bernard. *Arrogance: Rescuing America from the Media Elite.* New York: Warner Books, Inc., 2003.

Goldberg, Bernard. *Bias: A CBS Insider Exposes How the Media Distort the News.* Washington, D.C.: Regnery Publishing, Inc., 2002.

Patterson, Thomas. *Doing Well and Doing Good: How Soft News and Critical Journalism Are Shrinking the News Audience and Weakening Democracy—and What News Outlets Can Do about It.* Cambridge, Mass.: Harvard College, 2000.

Online

Gallup.com. The Gallup Organization. Multiple surveys.

People-press.org. The Pew Research Center for the People and the Press. Multiple surveys.

Sandy Davidson and Betty Winfield

Journalism
The Lifeblood of a Democracy

The story of American journalism is, like the story of the nation itself, a narrative of growth and change and struggle. Journalism's story is marked by a series of turning points, each of them opening the door to freedom a little wider for all Americans. Throughout history, journalists have risked prison and their purses to ensure that government officials conduct their business in public and that every citizen enjoys freedom of speech. The authors of this chapter are both professors at the Missouri School of Journalism. Dr. Sandra Davidson, who also has a law degree, teaches communication and media law. Dr. Betty Houchin Winfield is a Curators Professor who is a specialist in political communication and mass media history. She is the author and coauthor of numerous books and research studies.

In the American system of government, information is crucial for citizens to form enlightened opinions and to make informed political decisions. Founding father James Madison argued that a well-informed citizenry is necessary for a democracy: "A popular government without popular information is but a prologue to a farce, or a tragedy, or both." Madison further emphasized the important connection between public knowledge and a democracy by adding: "And a people who mean to be their own governors must arm themselves with the power which knowledge gives." Journalism provides the public information that is necessary for a democracy to thrive.

Journalism is a necessary conduit for not only spot news about what is happening within our society, but also what citizens think about what is happening. Because journalism is essential in a democracy, the United States provides a wide range of protections for citizens' right to know, to hear, to see, and to read information as well as to express their opinions.

18

Supreme Court Justice William O. Douglass once wrote that in centuries to come the United States will not be remembered for the vast technological inventions offered the world, but rather for its experiment with free expression.

This chapter recounts three centuries of stories that are building blocks for the country's historical and legal support for free expression. These personal accounts demonstrate in various ways the worth of journalism. Each person mentioned took tremendous risks to express opinions freely and to establish the public's right to know. Because the American Constitution and its Bill of Rights do not define who is a journalist, the right to share information and opinions belongs to everyone.

The Public's Historic Right to Know

When a popular coffeehouse owner attempted to publish the American colonies' first newspaper more than three hundred years ago, the Massachusetts colonial government stopped him. Benjamin Harris, a former London journalist, risked punishment for not having a license, the government's permission, to publish his *Public Occurrances, Both Forreign and Domestick.* In the September 25, 1690, issue, Harris promised accuracy—to take "pains he can to obtain a Faithful Relation of all things." Without any training except experience, Harris sought truth and proposed that "when there appears any material mistake in any thing that is collected, it shall be corrected." Harris also had a personal sense of social responsibility; he presented memorable occurrences so that "everyone might understand public affairs." Harris believed that the public had a right to know; his journalism would be the means.

His "occurrances" included regional events, such as fires and the health of the colony plagued with smallpox, flus, and fevers, as well as the strange disappearance of two local children. He pointed out societal dangers—the nearby "barbarous Indians" and shocking happenings on the European continent, including the French king's indecent liberties with his daughter-in-law.

How the public responded is not known, except by inference and by legal action taken against Harris. All of Harris's noble journalistic public goals and promises were for naught. The Massachusetts governor and council must have thought that the information he printed would be dangerous because four days after the first issue, they stopped Harris's journalistic efforts. Harris was presented with a restraining order with no explanation, except that he lacked a license to publish. Perhaps the officials interpreted stories of the children's disappearances and the "barbarous Indians" as criticism of their governance. Perhaps, too, the church leaders thought that the scandalous story about the French royalty was in bad taste. Although the colonial government restrained Harris's newspaper publication, the government did not imprison him. Harris, discouraged, returned to London.

While one colonial government stopped Benjamin Harris's newspaper, subsequent colonial printers continued to expose problems via their publications. They dared to criticize the government, despite risks to their safety.

One such printer was a New Yorker, John Peter Zenger.

The Right to Expose Government Corruption

Before the country's independence from Great Britain, ordinary citizens upheld the right to criticize officials. In 1735, a jury of his peers acquitted printer Zenger of the crime of "seditious libel"—the "crime" of criticizing government. Zenger had published an anonymous piece in the *New York Weekly Journal* that called the Crown's New York governor, William Cosby, a tyrant and oppressor. When Zenger refused to name Cosby's anonymous critics, prosecutors went after Zenger. At that time, truth was not a defense to seditious libel. The jury's role was only to decide if indeed Zenger had printed the words; the royal court judge would decide the far more important question of whether the words constituted seditious libel.

But Zenger's lawyer, Andrew Hamilton, argued, "Men who injure and oppress the people under their administration provoke them to cry out and complain, and then make that very complaint the foundation for new oppression and prosecutions." Hamilton told the jurors that they, not the judge, had the right to decide if Zenger was guilty. The jury agreed and acquitted Zenger.

How important was the *Zenger* case? The U.S. Supreme Court later called it "the earliest and most famous American experience with freedom of the press." Zenger's acquittal, the Court said, "set the colonies afire for its example of a jury refusing to convict a defendant of seditious libel against Crown authorities." Hamilton won the case not only for Zenger but also for the people's right to know what public officials were doing, as well as to express their opinions about the officials' performance.

Times of Stress: A Threat to the Right to Criticize

The right to know and to criticize continued to play important public roles not only during the colonial fight for independence but also afterward. By the late eighteenth century when the United States inaugurated its own self-government, Americans had experienced decades of expressing their political opinions and of even seeing harsh criticisms in the then very partisan press. The value of freedom of expression to the democracy was immense. Such freedom found its way into the country's constitution, approved with a Bill of Rights in 1791. The First Amendment says that "Congress shall make no law respecting an establishment of religion, or prohibiting the free exercise thereof; or abridging the freedom of speech, or of the press; or the right of the people peaceably to assemble, and to petition the Government for a redress of grievances." What exactly that meant for journalism in 1791 remains unclear, except that the phrases appeared to mean no licensing, which means no "prior restraint," such as what had stopped Benjamin Harris a century before. Still unclear legally for journalists was whether freedom of speech and press meant freedom from punishment for seditious libel, the crime of criticizing government.

In that embryonic national era, published viewpoints promoted both political discussion and involvement in the political process. Americans had access through the press to a multitude of ideas, representing various political factions and often leading to heated political debates. The press made no claim of fairness and objectivity and openly supported either the Federalist or the Anti-Federalist party, also called the Republicans. With no journalistic standard for balance in these partisan newspapers, the political information not only told what happened, but also recounted from a partisan viewpoint what writers thought about what was happening.

At the same time, the country's earliest political leaders attempted to manage public information through various kinds of economic support to favored printers, by their own essays written under pseudonyms, and with leaked and exclusive information. Although at times both personal and vicious attacks occurred, accounts in the political newspapers aided citizens' debates and involvement as the nation was being formed. For example, the Republican editors published scathing criticisms of President George Washington's policies and actions as being too kinglike and unseemly for a democracy. By the time of the second president, John Adams, in 1797, the country was facing a potential war with France and had become deeply divided over foreign policy. Following their own revolution in 1789, the

French began reestablishing a presence in North America and thus alarmed many Americans. In 1798, President Adams and his supporters pushed through a series of oppressive acts aimed at immigration and expression. The Federalists justified the Alien and Sedition Acts as a way to meet a serious foreign threat. The Alien Acts, aimed at French immigrants, increased the U.S. residency requirement for citizenship from five to fourteen years and allowed for imprisonment and selective deportation of noncitizens. The Sedition Act targeted critics of the administration and Republican editors, many of whom were supporters of France, as well as the Republican leaders, primarily Vice President Thomas Jefferson. The Sedition Act would fine and imprison anyone making "false, scandalous and malicious" statements against the government, the president, or either house of Congress.

Signed just seven years after the passage of the First Amendment, the Sedition Act was designed to inhibit the opposition press and challenge the public's right to criticize officials. The secretary of state spent half his time reading Anti-Federalist newspapers to ferret out sedition violators. The Federalists arrested twenty-five people and convicted ten, including a U.S. congressman, Matthew Lyon of Vermont, whose published letter accused President Adams of "ridiculous pomp, foolish adulation and selfish avarice." Fined one thousand dollars, Representative Lyon went to jail for four months. When an Anti-Federalist editor printed a lottery to raise money for Lyon's fine, he, too, was jailed for abetting a "criminal." Lyon's conviction became a cause célèbre. Vermont voters reelected Lyon to Congress by a two-to-one vote over his closest opponent.

A public uproar ensued as prosecutions continued for expressing opinions, whether orally or in written form. The acts became a contentious campaign issue during the presidential election in 1800. At that time, there was no judicial review. The Federalists lost the presidency and congressional seats. Adams was out, and opposition leader Thomas Jefferson became president. The acts expired the day before Jefferson's inauguration. He pardoned those in jail and canceled the remaining trials. By the new century, the public's right to have debates, even contentious ones on national and international issues, and the right to criticize its leaders had become more firmly established. Even controversial views would be tolerated, at least for a little while. Journalism would be the printed record of many controversial views about American social and political issues.

The Right to Express Even Hated Ideas

Opinions, even those expressing hated disclosures about societal injustices, are also a part of journalism. Publicly expressed viewpoints can reach an apex of controversy during times of great stress. By the mid-nineteenth century, the greatest stress occurred when the debate over slavery grew more and more heated throughout the nation. Such ever-widening national disagreement became a catalyst that eventually culminated in the Civil War. The abolition press had many Americans speaking and writing about this contentious issue of slavery, often at the expense of their own safety.

One who paid the highest price was Elijah Lovejoy, a former Presbyterian minister who established a reform and abolition newspaper, the *St. Louis Observer.* Lovejoy outraged St. Louis residents with his anti-Catholic editorials and attacks on local injustices, such as a district judge's leniency in the trial of persons accused of burning a black man alive. When the city council passed a resolution denying Lovejoy's free expression, he moved across the Mississippi River to Alton, Illinois. There, Lovejoy continued his crusade against slavery, only to have a mob destroy his office and printing press twice more. Ever determined, he persisted in his abolition stand after setting up his office a third time. Other newspapers wrote of Lovejoy's plight, and his unwavering stand became a national cause. Antislavery organizations garnered financial support for him. Still, a mob demolished his office once more and, in the process, killed him. Lovejoy had become a martyr for free expression. To advocate abolition became more than an antislavery crusade. It became advocacy of the right to express even unpopular opinions and survive.

After the Civil War, Ida B. Wells continued the crusade of Lovejoy and other abolitionists for equal rights. In Memphis, she used her newspaper *Free Speech* to rally African Americans against discrimination and to encourage them to boycott erring businesses or move to more race-friendly Oklahoma or Kansas. She kept exposing Memphis's injustices and denouncing the ever-growing numbers of lynchings, primarily in the heart of the South. When local citizens threatened her with violence and placed a bounty on her head, she moved to the safer North. Yet, like Lovejoy, Ida B. Wells persisted. For the next forty years, she publicized hundreds of lynchings.

Wells founded an Anti-Lynching Society, which she promoted for decades through articles, pamphlets, and hundreds of speeches throughout the country and in England. Her journalism created change. There were fewer lynchings, although they did not cease. Both Lovejoy's and Wells's efforts demonstrated that journalism could expose an injustice, rally the public, and alter a societal wrong.

The Duty to Investigate, Expose Wrongs, and Create Societal Change

By the early twentieth century, journalism became part of the reform movement to create change. Major societal issues included the Industrial Revolution, a large immigrant population, and the corporate nature of business, all affecting the well-being of Americans. Journalism, as part of the national progressive movement for political, economic, and social reform, addressed the urban, immigration, and industrialization problems.

Investigative journalists sought to publicly expose misconduct, vice, and corruption. Wearing proudly the derogatory label "Muckrakers," they exposed the meat-packing industry (Upton Sinclair); child labor (William Hard); the corruption in cities (Lincoln Steffens); abuses of workers (Ray Stannard Baker); the multimillion-dollar, patent-medicine businesses (Samuel Hopkins Adams); and even frauds in journalism (Will Irwin). Mostly writing in magazines for longer, more developed investigations or series, these journalistic reformers included premier writers and researchers. Foremost among them was Ida Tarbell, who did a series in *McClure's Magazine* on John D. Rockefeller and his monopolistic Standard Oil business abuses. In more than two thousand articles, the muckrakers' magazine exposures were fueled with indignation, energetically well-documented and convincing. Their journalistic efforts paid off, helping to gain the passage of the 1906 Pure Foods and Drug Act, more protective child labor laws, and increased antitrust legislation.

Today, despite so much of the country's mass media being tied to major corporations, the muckrakers' legacy lives. Journalists are calling society's attention to problems ranging from the Abu Ghraib tortures and Guantanamo Bay prisoner abuses to the country's air pollution, arsenic in the water supplies, tax unfairness, and workers' safety violations in Texas pipe manufacturing and West Virginia coal mines.

The Right to Free Expression during Wartime

In the United States, during wartime, free expression contracts. When under stress from an outside enemy, American society is less tolerant of those individuals who speak out and criticize the government's policies and practices. When there is national anxiety, journalists have more difficulty seeking and speaking truth about governmental actions. The casualties of war include freedoms of speech, press, and petition.

During World War I, Congress passed an Espionage Act in 1917 that criminalized free expression concerning the war, and amended that act with a Sedition Act in 1918 that went even further to inhibit speech and the press. Following World War I, the Supreme Court heard the first of the cases under these acts to test the limits of the First Amendment. In *Schenck v. United States* (1919), Justice Oliver Wendell Holmes said, "When a nation is at war many things that might be said in time of peace are such a hindrance to its effort that their utterance will not be endured so long as men fight." Charles Schenck, the general secretary of the Socialist party of the United States, had mailed leaflets to draft-age men, which told them that the draft violated the prohibition against involuntary servitude in the Thirteenth Amendment. Using Holmes's "clear and present danger" test, the Supreme Court upheld Schenck's conviction for conspiracy to obstruct military recruitment. "In impassioned language," the Court said, Schenck's writing "intimated that conscription was despotism in its worst form and a monstrous wrong against humanity in the interest of Wall Street's chosen few." Such language, the Court thought, constituted an unacceptable danger to the nation's war efforts.

A week later, the high court upheld the conviction of Eugene Debs, who ran for president five times on the Socialist ticket. In Ohio, Debs told a crowd that he had just returned from a prison where he was visiting three of his friends who had aided and abetted another friend in failing to register for the draft. He eulogized those three friends and said he was proud of them. He told the jury trying him: "I have been accused of obstructing the war. I admit it. Gentlemen, I abhor war. I would oppose the war if I stood alone." Two years later, a presidential order released Debs from his ten-year sentence.

In another World War I case, *Abrams v. United States,* the high Court upheld the convictions of five defendants who had been born in Russia. They had thought that a U.S. military expedition sent to Siberia to attack the Germans from the east was instead an attempt to crush the Russian revolution. They wrote two leaflets that asked for the end of producing bullets, bayonets, and cannons. At the time, calling for curtailment of production of necessary war materials was a federal offense. The five were convicted of conspiracy to encourage resistance to the war with Germany—even though they had written, "We hate and despise German militarism more than do you hypocritical tyrants."

They received sentences of twenty years. Finally, Holmes's gag reflex had been activated, and the "Great Dissenter" penned one of his greatest dissents: " . . . when men have realized that time has upset many fighting faiths, they may come to believe . . . that the ultimate good desired is better reached by *free trade in ideas*—that the best test of truth is the power of the thought to get itself accepted in the *competition of the market.*"

Holmes's legal view was half a century ahead of his time. The people who expressed dissenting viewpoints to an unpopular war had risked imprisonment and were convicted. Their courageous efforts eventually helped protect even unpopular expressions during wartime.

Journalism's Duty to Criticize for the Benefit of Democracy

Especially in times of turmoil, the press has a *duty* to criticize public officials for the benefit of democracy. The Supreme Court made this clear in 1931 when the country was suffering extreme economic hardship. The United States had endured World War I and the great stock market crash of 1929. The Great Depression and Prohibition were in full swing, along with bootlegging gangsters such as Al Capone and Bugsy Malone. Some public officials undoubtedly were on the gangsters' payrolls.

Jay Near and his partner used the *Saturday Press* to charge that Minneapolis government officials, including the police chief, were in cahoots with local gangsters. After the paper's first issue, gangsters shot but did not kill Near's partner. Near wrote that the prosecuting attorney was not doing enough to clean up the situation. Not surprisingly, Near's public declaration so angered the prosecuting attorney that he sought to close the newspaper under the Minnesota nuisance statute that permitted shutting down any "malicious, scandalous and defamatory newspaper." The trial judge ordered Near to close his newspaper or be fined and then jailed for up to a year. Upon appeal, the U.S. Supreme Court ruled that the prior restraint authorized by the Minnesota statute was inconsistent with liberty of the press.

Given the backdrop of the Prohibition era, the U.S. Supreme Court declared that "the administration of government has become more complex, the opportunities for malfeasance and corruption have multiplied, crime has grown to most serious proportions, and the danger . . . emphasizes the primary need of a vigilant and courageous press, especially in great cities."

Although the decision was 5 to 4, *Near v. Minnesota* has withstood the test of time. Instead of permitting restraint of the press, the Court encouraged the press to be "courageous and vigilant," not timid or intimidated. The First Amendment's "chief purpose," according to the Court, was "to prevent previous restraint upon publication." The Court also used another term for previous restraint—"censorship." Although the Court did not go so far as saying the press could never be censored, it made clear that prior restraint could only occur in "exceptional cases" involving obscenity or some areas of national security, such as the movement of troops during wartime. Later, the Court added that the press could occasionally be restrained to ensure a defendant a fair trial.

Nevertheless, the "character and conduct" of public officers, such as the Minnesota city officials, "remain open to debate and free discussion in the press," the Court declared. If a newspaper made false accusations, the public officer would just have to use the libel laws.

Thus, an uncensored press, unleashed from prior restraint, is at least free if not duty-bound to be "courageous and vigilant" in exposing governmental corruption, but the press must attempt to give truthful accounts.

Protection from Libel Suits

During another period of great societal unrest, the 1960s civil rights movement, oral and written expressions in the South became quite contentious. To speak for equality in many Southern regions meant facing the same kinds of violent reactions as did Ida B. Wells and Elijah Lovejoy a century before. This time the issue was school integration. Following the Supreme Court ruling in *Brown v. Board of Education* (1954) that separate schools were not equal, civil rights workers risked their lives to integrate public schools. The public debates became heated, and Southern newspapers that supported integration were boycotted and speakers were jailed.

One such reaction caused the U.S. Supreme Court to greatly change the nation's libel law concerning public officials. The case involved the *New York Times,* which had published a political advertisement, "Heed Their Rising Voices," written by a civil rights group protesting brutal police treatment of Montgomery, Alabama, college students and the Rev. Dr. Martin Luther King, Jr. The copy did contain some factual errors. L. B. Sullivan, the Montgomery police commissioner, took offense at what he considered to be personal criticism, although he was not identified by name. Sullivan sued for libel and won $500,000. The *Times* appealed the judgment.

In 1964, the Supreme Court ruled in favor of the newspaper in the landmark case of *New York Times Co. v. Sullivan,* emphasizing that the press could be *wrong* when criticizing public officials for official conduct and still receive First Amendment protection. Libel cases had become too easy for public officials to win in court and could create a "chilling" effect on the media, the Court thought. So the Court decided to thaw public debate on public issues by making it much more difficult for public officials to win libel suits. As a result of this ruling, public officials must prove the media acted with "actual malice"—"knowledge that a statement is false, or reckless disregard of whether it is true or false."

In curbing public officials' ability to win libel cases, the Court spoke of "a profound national commitment to the principle that debate on public issues should be uninhibited, robust, and wide-open." The Court also spoke of the necessity of providing "breathing space": "[E]rroneous statement is inevitable in free debate, and . . . it must be protected if the freedoms of expression are to have the 'breathing space' that they need to survive."

In short, freedom to criticize public officials includes freedom to err— so long as the errors are not intentional or reckless. The threat of libel actions cannot be used to stifle critical comments about public officials. Three years later, the Supreme Court extended the "actual malice" requirement to public figures, again giving leeway to the press. Today, a president, governor, or mayor finds it mighty difficult to sue for libel, even if the statement is exaggerated about the official's fitness for office, conduct in office, moral character, private sexual conduct, or close connections with industry. Some say that journalists sometimes go too far and do not check their facts carefully enough and that too many mistakes are made, yet leeway for the press means that the debate involving public officials, public actions, and public decisions will be robust.

The Triumph of the Right to Know over Secrecy

The right to know what is happening in a democracy is constantly tested during wartime. While the Vietnam War raged on in 1971, a reporter from the *New York Times* received photocopies of a secret forty-seven-volume study of the history of the U.S. involvement in Vietnam, commonly known as the "Pentagon Papers." Prepared by the Defense Department, the study was to be kept secret, but one of the authors, former Pentagon employee Daniel Ellsberg, had turned against the war and leaked copies to the *Times.*

On June 13, a Sunday, the *Times* printed its first story in a series based on the "Pentagon Papers." Less than forty-eight hours later, the newspaper received a telegram from the U.S. attorney general, John Mitchell, saying that any more Pentagon Papers articles would bring about "irreparable injury to the defense interests of the United States." The *Times* did not bow to the attorney general and instead shared its story with the *Washington Post*. A lower court that had issued a temporary restraining order to stop the *Times* rescinded the order four days later. Judge Murray Gurfein wrote, "These are troubled times. There is no greater safety valve for discontent and cynicism about the affairs of Government than freedom of expression in any form. This has been the genius of our institutions throughout our history." Immediately, a federal appeals court reversed Judge Gurfein's decision and demanded further hearings before the *Times* printed any more of its Pentagon Papers series.

In tribute to the importance the Supreme Court places on attempts to shut down the press, the Court heard arguments in the case on June 26, 1971, just thirteen days after the first story ran. The Court issued its decision only four days later. The government's argument could not stand because the government could not prove how the Pentagon Papers breached national security. The Court ruled for freedom of the press, even during wartime, and gave the message that the people had the right to know how their country got involved in war without having to wait until the war was over. In this case, freedom of the press prevailed over the government's feeble claims of national security. The newspapers could and did print the history of that long and agonizing Vietnam War.

The People's Right to Know Political Extremes

A pioneer broadcaster, Edward R. Murrow, was known for setting a standard of the best of broadcast news for almost twenty years. During World War II, Murrow's "This . . . Is London" CBS updates brought the Battle of Britain into American living rooms. During the Cold War, in television documentaries on the show *See It Now,* Murrow and his coproducer, Fred Friendly, examined various Cold War issues, among them the tactics of Senator Joseph McCarthy, who for four years made charges without supporting evidence. McCarthy timed his accusations to correspond with immediate deadlines, meaning that the press had no time to investigate his charges. The senator alleged that there were hundreds of Communists in the State Department and, later, the rest of the government, including individual

Army officers. The press dutifully reported his statements and speeches, which he paced so that rebuttals and denials never caught up with the stories.

On March 9, 1954, Murrow devoted an entire *See It Now* program to Senator McCarthy's accusations and tactics, using McCarthy's own words. Murrow took a great risk when he dared to speak out at a time when few yet opposed the senator publicly, including the president. The broadcaster concluded his devastating portrait of the senator's actions with these words:

> We will not be driven by fear into an age of unreason if we dig deep in our history and our doctrine, and remember that we are not descended from fearful men who feared to write, to speak, to associate and to defend causes that were for the moment unpopular. This is no time for men who oppose Senator McCarthy's methods to keep silent. . . . We can deny our heritage and our history, but we cannot escape responsibility for the result.

On April 6, McCarthy responded to Murrow's *See It Now* program with accusations about the broadcaster, but they did not resonate.

The subsequent Army-McCarthy hearings allowed TV cameras and microphones to bring the public face to face with McCarthy's tactics of character assassination. McCarthy lost credibility and the Senate later censored him. Journalism had helped the public see the contradictions of the senator's media manipulations and abusive power.

So What Good Is Journalism?

The long journalism journey from 1690, when the Massachusetts colonial government shut down Benjamin Harris's newspaper, is marked by journalists who strove to inform citizens about what officials were doing, who warned of dangers to the country's ideals, who investigated potential wrongdoings, and who advocated reform.

Journalists who have provided the news about government and stood up to tyranny, slavery, and corrupt officials have given Americans the information they need to judge their rulers and make decisions. Some have sacrificed their safety and their lives for their principles. All have advanced the cause of the people's right to know and have access to information, as well as the country's freedom of expression.

Journalism is the lifeblood of democracy. Journalism is a necessary condition for the United States' form of government. It keeps information flowing, nourishing all segments of society from the single individual to the body politic. If the flow of information from journalists stopped, then what would result? Madison said it best—"a farce, or a tragedy, or perhaps both."

Sources

You can learn more about the people and the cases who have made history in these readings.

James Madison
Padover, Saul K. *The Complete Madison.* Millwood, N.Y.: Kraus Reprint Co., 1953. (See especially: James Madison to W. T. Barry, August 4, 1822, on p. 337.)

Benjamin Harris
Bailyn, Bernard. *The Ideological Origins of the American Revolution.* Cambridge, Mass.: Belknap Press of Harvard University Press, 1967.

Clark, Charles E., David Paul Nord, Gerald Baldasty, Michael Schudson, and Loren Ghiglione. *Three Hundred Years of the American Newspaper.* Worcester, Mass.: American Antiquarian Society, 1991.

Martin, Robert W. T. *The Free and Open Press: The Founding of American Democratic Press Liberty, 1640–1800.* New York: New York University Press, 2001.

Smith, Jeffrey A. *Printers and Press Freedom: The Ideology of Early American Journalism.* New York: Oxford University Press, 1988.

John Peter Zenger
Cheslau, Irving G. *John Peter Zenger and the "New-York Weekly Journal": A Historical Study.* New York: Zenger Memorial Fund, 1952.

Katz, Stanley Nider, ed. *A Brief Narrative of the Case and Trial of John Peter Zenger, Printer of the* New York Weekly Journal. 2nd ed. Cambridge, Mass.: Belknap Press of Harvard University Press, 1972.

Konkle, Burton A. *The Life of Andrew Hamilton, 1676–1741.* Philadelphia: National Pub. Co., 1941.

Alien and Sedition Acts
Levy, Leonard W. *Emergence of a Free Press.* New York and Oxford: Oxford University Press, 1985.

Miller, John C. *Crisis in Freedom: The Alien and Sedition Acts.* Boston: Little Brown, 1951.

Smith, James Morton. *Freedom's Fetters: The Alien and Sedition Laws and American Civil Liberties.* Ithaca, N.Y.: Cornell University Press, 1956.

Tigg, James. *Benjamin Franklin Bache and the* Philadelphia Aurora. Philadelphia: University of Pennsylvania Press, 1991.

Ida B. Wells-Barnett

Royster, Jacqueline Hone, ed. *Southern Horrors and Other Writings: The Anti-Lynching Campaign of Ida B. Wells, 1892–1900.* Boston: Bedford Books, 1997.

Streitmatter, Roger. *Raising Her Voice: African-American Journalists Who Changed History.* Lexington: University Press of Kentucky, 1994.

Elijah Lovejoy

Gill, John. *Tide without Turning: Elijah P. Lovejoy and Freedom of the Press.* Boston: Beacon Press, 1958.

Walters, Ronald G. *The Antislavery Appeal: American Abolitionism after 1830.* Baltimore: Johns Hopkins University Press, 1976.

Muckrakers

Chalmers, David. *The Social and Political Ideas of the Muckrakers.* New York: Citadel Press, 1964.

Filler, Louis. *The Muckrakers.* University Park: Pennsylvania State University Press, 1976.

Weinberg, Arthur, and Lila Shaffer Weinberg, eds. *The Muckrakers.* New York: Simon and Schuster, 1961.

World War I, Espionage and Sedition Acts

Schenck v. United States, 249 U.S. 47 (1919).

Debs v. United States, 249 U.S. 211 (1919).

Abrams v. United States, 250 U.S. 616 (1919).

Chafee, Zechariah, Jr. *Free Speech in the United States.* Cambridge, Mass.: Harvard University Press, 1941.

Vaughn, Stephen. *Holding Fast the Inner Lines: Democracy, Nationalism, and the Committee on Public Information.* Chapel Hill: University of North Carolina Press, 1980.

Jay Near

Near v. Minnesota, 283 U.S. 697 (1931).

Friendly, Fred. *Minnesota Rag: The Dramatic Story of the Landmark Supreme Court*

Case that Gave New Meaning to Freedom of the Press. New York: Random House, 1981.

New York Times Co. v. Sullivan
New York Times Co. v. Sullivan, 376 U.S. 254 (1964).
Lewis, Anthony. *Make No Law: The Sullivan Case and the First Amendment.* New York: Random House, 1991.

Pentagon Papers Case
New York Times Co. v. United States, 403 U.S. 713 (1971).
United States v. New York Times Co., 328 F. Supp. 324 (S.D.N.Y. 1971).
Salisbury, Harrison. *Without Fear or Favor: The* New York Times *and Its Times.* New York: Times, 1980.
Ungar, Sanford J. *The Papers and the Papers: An Account of the Legal and Political Battle over the Pentagon Papers.* New York: Dutton, 1972.

Edward R. Murrow
Murrow, Edward R. *In Search of Light: The Broadcasts of Edward R. Murrow, 1938–1961.* New York: Alfred A. Knopf, 1967.
Sperber, Ann M. *Murrow: His Life and Times.* New York: Freundlich, 1986.

NPR Offers News and Companionship

In this era of shrinking audiences and growing cynicism, National Public Radio stands as evidence that Americans still value honest and thoughtful storytelling. Just as the respondents to the national survey suggested, the example of NPR shows that there is strong and growing demand for journalism based on accurate reporting and well-reasoned commentary. It also shows that good journalism thrives when profit pressures and partisanship are absent. Geneva Overholser holds the Hurley Chair at the Missouri School of Journalism. She is a former editor of the Des Moines Register *and former ombudsman of the* Washington Post.

My mother's name was Betty Moore. *She was murdered by her boyfriend with a butcher knife right in front of me when I was five years old. He stabbed her in the heart, so she was just bleeding to death. She wanted to reach out to me but couldn't.*

March 13, 2003. The Beltway's a logjam. Gray sheets of rain slap the windshield. A dull ache blooms mid-forehead. Forty miles more to the airport. And I'm listening to *this?*

All her blood was just like covering the ground. I'm talking about a big puddle. I watched her, you know. I looked in her eyes, and, I mean, just watching all of that life just disappear. And you just knowing this woman ain't gonna never hold me again.

This voice—haunting, compelling, recounting a life so far from mine—is coming from *All Things Considered.* And, despite the rain, the traffic, the headache, I stay with it. I'm hooked. So are twenty-six million people weekly, an audience that has doubled in the last decade, even as newspaper readership and network news viewership has plummeted, even as most of radio has virtually deserted news. NPR, once so dependent on federal funding that its very existence was serially threatened by Congress's mood shifts, is now a stable $150 million business, generously supported by its listeners, as well as by foundations and corporations. Why, even its former nemesis Newt Gingrich is now a fan: "It's one of the great mysteries of how life evolves that I now find myself driving to work listening routinely every morning to NPR."

American media are in crisis, most of them bleeding readers, listeners, viewers—and credibility and influence. Journalists despair. Consumers deplore. Pundits sneer. A nation that's never needed more urgently to see complex and difficult truths has media that have never sought so zealously to make money—more and more of it every quarter. In a globalizing world, many of the news links that bind this nation, this sole superpower, to the rest of humanity grow steadily weaker. And then there is NPR, a network grown from ninety member stations in 1970 to more than nine hundred in 2005. In the last decade, its staff has nearly doubled. It has bureaus and offices in thirty-six locations throughout the country and abroad.

In the last five years alone, the number of listeners to NPR stations has increased by 54 percent, and its ardent fans say life without *All Things Considered* and *Morning Edition* is unimaginable. They'll tell you that NPR went with them to college and that it brings them home every night. They say it gave them topics to discuss early in their marriages, that its principals are role models, that it brought genuineness where other media only postured. They thank NPR for small joys and everyday companionship, and for guiding them through the nation's triumphs and tragedies.

Consider Dennis Germenis, a forty-six-year-old, married insurance salesman from Texas, a church choir director and freelance musician (and fisherman). He reads his local paper and watches the ten o'clock news, but, he says, "I have been listening to NPR since 1981. You can listen while you eat, while you get dressed, when you're driving. I like how NPR lets me know what's going on around the world as well as our nation. I like how they give me the headlines, and then they go in depth to give me the details. They also give me both sides of the issue."

Or consider David Teague, a retired professor in western North Carolina, who calls his NPR affiliate "an oasis in a vast wasteland." He loves the music, but he depends on the news coverage. "It ranges from international down to the local. It has human interest, commentary that is from both the right and the left, but the commentary from each is intelligent, reasoned commentary. The positions taken are supported by fact and reason. I hate being yelled at, and most commercial TV and radio stations do that with distressing regularity. I contribute to my public radio station, regularly, and I am only sorry the amount cannot be more."

What makes NPR so different from other media? For one thing, it doesn't aim to make a profit. For another, it is mission-driven, with public service at its core. Newspapers typically get 85 percent of their revenue from advertising, commercial broadcasts virtually 100 percent. NPR, a nonprofit organization, is in substantial part listener-supported. As its then ombudsman, Jeffrey Dvorkin, says: "This curious economic model has made this happen. The pledge drives—people complain about them constantly, but they've created a listener response that is very powerful: *This is coming out of my wallet, so I feel differently about it than if I were sitting there watching ads for Ford pickup trucks.*"

At a time when other media are doing fine at staying in business, but not so well at staying in journalism, NPR has a leg up in this quest. But the difference goes deeper, still. In interviews with dozens of staffers, and the listeners they serve, four characteristics emerged as primary explanations for NPR's uniqueness: the medium itself, its mission, its structure, and competition.

The Medium

Susan Stamberg says it's the power of radio. "With our news stories, you can hear the tanks yourself. And you get the power of the voice, in a way that puts you in the presence of the person. And (she winks at this inveterately print-oriented journalist) we don't get our quotes wrong."

When Stamberg smiles, her eyes, her cheeks—her *voice*—smile, and her smile pours out of the radio. "She's got air presence off the air. She is authentic. She has this insatiable curiosity that is expressed on the air. She gave a voice to the ideas, and people gravitated to her." That's what Bill Siemering, the original director of programming for NPR, says. Not that this pioneer woman anchor of a national news show was an immediate success. When first she spoke out on *All Things Considered (ATC)* in early 1972, program managers griped: "Bill, the high frequencies in women's voices just don't translate well. Women can do the soft features, not the news. They just don't sound authoritative."

Poor benighted managers. Accustomed to broadcaster-speak—to *announcing*. To people talking *at* their listeners. And here was Stamberg, straightforward and relaxed, talking *with* them. "The very best writing for radio is like clear water," says Linda Wertheimer, a thirty-five-year NPR veteran. "It's simple and unadorned." NPR talk is conversational, written for the ear—for listeners in intimate spaces: bedrooms, cars, kitchens, offices. The voices bring the stories home to us.

Wertheimer sits in an office as cozy and personal as NPR's sprawling Massachusetts Avenue building is businesslike. She tells me, "Radio gets right in there. Radio wakes you up in the morning. You talk to the radio." And the talk it delivers is straight from the original source. "What we do here is we use the best tape. I don't try to hammer them into my narrative. We use the best thing they said." Read a story in the *New York Times* about a survey of public opinion, and you may just skip the quotes. Listen to an NPR story about the same survey, and the story IS the quotes.

> Pops sitting on the toilet, needle in his arm,
> Spoon still warm,
> Full of heroin and charm

Like print, radio encourages active reflectiveness: Without pictures, you must shape the story in your own mind. Yet radio has broadcast's immediacy. Siemering—in many ways the father of NPR—will tell you about the day, early in his career, when his station brought in live lines from all over town and mixed them into a nonstop composition of steel-cutting saws and workers leaving their shifts, airplanes landing, and "a musical bell-like machine at General Mills." A celebration of sound, the piece made listeners aware of the sounds of the city around them. Stamberg talks about the time she was set to interview the great jazzman Dave Brubeck. The studio had no piano, so she took him home to her upright. During the interview, she asked Brubeck how he got into music. He spoke of growing up on a cattle ranch, "riding horseback hours a day, alone" and often pumping water for the cattle. "And the gasoline engines go chug/chug/chug/chug/khBOME/khBOME/khBOME/khCHUG/khKAKAKAKAKAKA/kaGOWG/kaGOWG, and they go on like this for hours." And on the program, these engine sounds begin to blend with Brubeck's "Quartet" and "Take Five."

Even radio's limits can become strengths. After the horrific events of September 11, 2001, the visual impact began to wear—the awful fall of the towers, again and again, no ceasing, no solace. Stamberg decided NPR should create a refuge. "I was getting more and more miserable. This relentless wash of misery that only made you want to hole up somewhere. I thought to myself: 'What can I do?' And I thought: 'Stop the programs and do musical interludes.' I went to some of our greatest artists and said, 'What should we be listening to?' Leonard Slatkin picked Aaron Copeland's 'Appalachian Spring'; Beverly Sills, an aria from *Norma*; Billy Joel, 'New York State of Mind.' I've never seen an outpouring like that. It got to all these things we talk about here: Reaching people at their emotional centers."

The Mission

If Stamberg thinks it's the medium itself that distinguishes NPR, Jay Kernis would say it's the culture. The legacy. "We understand what the mission is, and we think it's valuable," he says, pulling out of his wallet a well-worn, laminated rectangle. He regards it earnestly. "We believe," he says, "that this actually makes a difference in people's lives." "This" is a condensed version of the principles that drive NPR. And Kernis, who started out in public radio as a sixteen-year-old, is a true believer. The creator of *Morning Edition,* he is now senior vice president for programming, and the difference the principles make in his life is evident: Other media executives in like positions would be talking to a reporter about penetration and market reach, net income before taxes and responsibility to shareholders. Kernis talks about idealism, the power to help find solutions, respect for the listener, attention to detail.

To explain, we return to Bill Siemering, whose vision lives on at NPR today. Siemering got into radio in college, then became manager of a student station at SUNY Buffalo. There, in 1969, he opened a storefront studio in the black community—an experience that transformed him. "The culture was turning over," he says. "That's why I knew we needed to include the worlds of art and culture. If Nixon had been listening to the songs people were singing, maybe he wouldn't have been so surprised" to see thousands of protesters in front of the White House.

Siemering was taken by the rich vibrancy of the black community—and by its virtual invisibility in the news. Oh, there'd be the occasional story about problems in the local school—the thin visible layer of a problem three hundred years in the making. But nothing delving into the real lives he saw before him. Same with student protests. Here would be the real event, the painfully passionate, questing crowd of young people. And there would be the coverage—all broken windows, and fearful judgments—no connection, no effort to get inside, to understand or explain. "I'm not talking about right or wrong," he says. "I'm talking about different perceptions of reality based on different experiences."

And the places you will hear called hell
Those are the places I've stayed in.
And places where you won't ever have to sleep,
Those are the places I've laid on . . .

Siemering thought radio could help bridge the gap. He poured his experiences into a groundbreaking essay, published in November 1969: "Public Radio: Some Essential Ingredients." Commercial media, he wrote, are "utility grade meat, devoid of taste and low in nutrition. The plastic, faceless morning men, afternoon men and night men who recycle like a cartridge tape can be plugged into any city. They do not give us a sense of the individual community." Then a statement as lamentably fresh today as when he wrote it: "In an age of the information overload, we need a broader definition of local news than one confined to auto accidents, fire and muggings; we need a more accurate barometer of what the public wants than top 40 charts and sales of cigarettes. Thus far, the media have presented the world from a single perspective, and they have viewed political and social minorities as a spectator views animals in a zoo."

The young radio innovator's "Essential Ingredients" soon became the raw material for the original NPR mission and goals statement. Siemering wrote of a network that would "promote personal growth rather than corporate gains; it will regard individual differences with respect and joy rather than derision and hate; it will celebrate the human experience as infinitely varied rather than vacuous and banal; it will encourage a sense of active constructive participation, rather than apathetic helplessness." NPR would enable listeners to be more responsive, better informed, more engaged in their communities and their world. "That was thirty years ago," says Wertheimer, "and we're still doing it."

One of the principles is to keep citizenship squarely in mind. "Public broadcasting . . . must supply the basic nutrients to save the life of the public from information starvation," Siemering had written in "Public Broadcasting." The first broadcast network coverage of a Senate debate live was NPR's 1978 presentation of the Panama Canal Treaty debate. NPR brought us also Linda Wertheimer's incisive reporting on the Nixon impeachment and Nina Totenberg's riveting coverage of the Anita Hill/Clarence Thomas controversy. And, when America's troops bore down on Baghdad in the spring of 2003, NPR's Anne Garrels was one of a handful of correspondents there to report on their arrival. In a March 31 interview with Garrels, Bob Edwards—then host of *Morning Edition*—asked her what restraints faced the press in Baghdad: "A lot. The press corps is now only about 150 reporters from around the world, and there are only 16 Americans. Apart from freelancers, the networks are absent, as is CNN. We all live in one of two hotels, and since the information ministry was bombed, we now work out of the Palestine Hotel under very strict surveillance of Iraqi security."

Then there's the commitment to speak with many voices. "To allow minority views to be unrepresented or misrepresented is to deny freedom of choice and threaten the life of the democracy," Siemering wrote. The first words on the very first *ATC* program were those of a black nurse talking about her heroin addiction: "Harry coming knockin' at your door," she said in tones seductive and alluring enough to make addiction seem real. Siemering wanted to put the listener right there with the person speaking. Not in the studio, but out on the streets, in the homes, of those whose experiences he or she was hearing.

This was my world, this was where I lived. This was what we were living, this is what this book is about. And I ain't never touched something this close to what I know and what I've seen in my life. I didn't believe nobody could even write down what we were living. I didn't even know what we were living wasn't supposed to really be.

Let other journalists walk the same rutted paths, thought Siemering. People want to be exposed to lives they would never come into contact with otherwise. "If you can establish trust, you can take 'em by the hand, and lead 'em to new things, and they'll be interested in those new things."

Another value at NPR is a constructive emphasis. Where other media tear down, NPR has sought to be not only empowering, but even ennobling. When the late CBS journalist Charles Kuralt first heard *ATC* in a country store in Virginia, he said: "Its words are well-chosen, and the voices that speak them are calm. The program has an air of reason and good humor about it, and hopefulness. . . . I bet that man and his daughter in the store where I bought the cheese and apples listen to *All Things Considered* not only because it informs them but also because it makes them feel better. It makes me feel better, too. It makes me feel better about the world by confirming, from time to time, that there is cause for cautious optimism or even for celebration."

Reading helped me to survive through a lot of my childhood. It was a place to go when I didn't want to be where I was at. You know, I could open this book and climb into the pages and disappear.

"It's the way the stories are told, the depth and the level of them, which attracts people who will stay with us," says Stamberg. "It's about how we view our listeners, which is unusual in broadcasting. We really do assume they are intelligent—or at least extremely curious—and they want to know things. That we're all in the same boat, and on this voyage together."

For Wertheimer—who says, "I have always tried to talk to people about what THEY think about events"—this NPR commitment to telling complex stories out in the communities where they are lived through real lives has produced countless memorable moments, which are reflected in the pictures and memorabilia that make her small office so vivid. She thinks of how Ada, Oklahoma, provided the vehicle for a look at the American economy in the form of "the nineties visited on this one little town." "That was an outstanding piece of reporting about what's happening to millions of workers and how their misery is brought about," a Los Angeles reader responded.

She thinks of the Second Baptist Church of Houston, which, in 1995, gave NPR a chance to look at the underreported phenomenon of religious change in America. "America is an amazingly God-fearing place. They think of newspaper people as godless. Whenever we do a piece, we do it with respect. I thought a lot of what people told me [she mentions the notion that churches have become "doctrine-free"] was completely incredible. But I just reported it." Scott Wright of Walnut Ridge, Arkansas, noted this respectful tone when he wrote to say, "Thank you for your story on exciting Second. I am pleased that fundamental religion, even as nontraditional as Ed Young's church, can be treated fairly in the media. I am not given to much that fundamentalist Christianity stands for, yet I think there might even be a place for me at Second Baptist Houston." Paul and Ruth Andrexall of Ardin, North Carolina, e-mailed: "Thanks for tonight's segment on the Second Baptist Church of Houston. Although we do not share all aspects of Second Baptist's philosophy, we were pleased that you aired the segment and treated the subject fairly."

In a world of charge and countercharge about media bias, distortion, and slant, Wertheimer's philosophy is this: "I tend to have a really kind of simple notion: Show up. Look at what you're looking at. Come back and say what you saw."

My name is Yanier Franklin Donald Moore, but everybody knows me as Blak. I was born April 24, 1971, in Cooke County Hospital, in Chicago, Illinois. I'm 31 years old approaching 32, and there were times I didn't think I would live to see the age of 16 or 18 or 21, but here I am.

For all the constancy of NPR's mission, it is not a static thing. The mission statement is periodically rewritten and has now been joined by something called "Core Values," essentially identified by listeners. Under categories like "Qualities of the Mind" come values such as "Love of lifelong learning. Substance. Curiosity. Credibility. Accuracy. Honesty." There are also Qualities of the Heart and Spirit and Qualities of Craft. Says Siemering: "As it works out, and I find this most fascinating, the core values that the listeners identified correlate very well with the original mission statement. Which is proof that these are not just some notions or ideals, but that they actually drive the work and are recognized by the listeners through the programming."

Jay Kernis, he of the much-loved mission statement, left NPR in 1987 to go to CBS television. He stayed fourteen years, including five years as a producer at the hugely successful and respected *60 Minutes,* before returning to NPR in 2001, leaving his family in New York. "I loved being at CBS. Certainly the pay was better. Don Hewitt (the program's creator) always said he had the best job in American journalism—part Ed Murrow and part Ed Sullivan, searching for good stories and telling them in the most compelling way." Still, says Kernis, he'd listen to NPR with envy. "Too many times, in television, it is 'This is the way we do it.' Or, the paycheck. Or, 'It'll get a good rating.' At NPR, we know why we're here.

"And the work has great meaning."

The Structure

The effect of this legacy—this history—at NPR is that somebody different is in the driver's seat. That's the distinguishing characteristic that Ellen Weiss would cite. Intense and engaging, Weiss is a behind-the-scenes power in a long-sleeved T-shirt and jeans. She is senior editor of the national desk, overseeing all domestic coverage for all programs, and to interview her is to see a parade of staffers seeking her counsel, and to hear a constantly ringing phone. Amid the chaos, Weiss takes time to make the case that the question of who is in charge is critically important. "We are listener-driven. We wouldn't exist without member stations. Our listeners feel like they're the owners."

Siemering concurs: "You have to be significantly different to have people voluntarily give you money, and yet you have to be engagingly presented so that people will listen and stations will buy the programming."

It wasn't always thus. Back in its beginning, NPR was mostly government-funded with the money coming to it directly from the Corporation for Public Broadcasting. Two powerful changes came in the mid-eighties. The CPB began routing its support primarily through member stations. And another public radio network was born, known today as Public Radio International (PRI). Both are distributors of programming. NPR, for example, distributes its own shows, such as *ATC* and *Morning Edition,* along with member-station programs like *Fresh Air* from Philadelphia's WHYY. PRI is primarily a distributor, providing its member stations with the BBC World Service, for example, as well as *Marketplace,* which is produced by member station Minnesota Public Radio in association with the University of Southern California. Minnesota Public Radio has created its own distribution network, American Public Media, to take advantage of new broadcast and digital platforms. NPR controls no airtime on its member stations, which offer program schedules that make the most sense for each city or region. Today's competitive situation puts the reins in the hands of member stations, each of which buys the programs it wants from NPR and from other producers, distributors, and independent companies.

Meanwhile, as competition arose, public funding shrank dramatically, and corporate and foundation support grew. Now, says Ken Stern, NPR's executive vice president, of the network's $136 million annual budget, about half comes from member stations—meaning, for the most part, from listeners. A quarter comes from corporate sponsors—those testimonies of excellence to some product or principle now inserted here and there throughout the programming. Twenty percent or so comes from foundations and other types of grants, and the rest is miscellaneous. The only direct government funding comes through competitive grants from agencies such as the National Science Foundation or the National Endowment for the Arts, for specific programming. It constitutes about 2 percent of the total revenues.

Having gone through life-threateningly shaky times in its three decades—particularly because of its early reliance on tax money—NPR is a "far more stable business than we used to be," says Stern. A 2003 bequest of $240 million from philanthropist Joan Kroc has further assured that stability, and enabled NPR to expand its news capabilities as well as to deepen its online presence. In addition, corporate sponsorships are easier to get than they used to be—a fact that does not look so positive to everyone. Indeed, the late Richard Salant, former president of CBS News and a member of NPR's board in the eighties, resigned to protest reliance on grants earmarked for particular news coverage—on Japan, say, or on environmental issues—citing the potential for unacceptable influence on the choice of news topics.

One reason companies like to sponsor NPR programming is that the audience has what's seen in the media trade as desirable demographics. It's educated, engaged, motivated, and influential. Audience research shows that more than 60 percent have a college degree or beyond, and 80 percent vote. NPR listeners are active in their communities, enthusiastic consumers of the arts, and big on things like dining out—and buying books. Dan Schorr, who has a contract with NPR as a senior commentator, says: "When I wrote my own memoirs and talked to the public relations people about plugging the book, about trying to arrange interviews with me, I said, 'I don't know if it's worth much to you, but I could probably arrange something on NPR.' Their answer: 'On the list of major places to go to when you have a book, the number one single thing that sells more books than any other is *Morning Edition.*'"

No matter how I had to get the light, I mean I would read by the light of the street light, streaming through the window. I would read by candlelight, by flashlight, however—it didn't make a difference—I was gonna read.

In a media world in which newspapers are routinely pressed to return 20 percent profit margins and higher, and broadcast outlets well upward of that, NPR's relative independence of market pressures is remarkable—and not just for the absence of profit pressure. NPR's independence allows it to keep out of several common media ruts. Acknowledging the woes of many a journalist friend, Ellen Weiss talks about the "incredible honor and privilege of working in a place where you really do feel that there is a freedom of ideas." Says Wertheimer: "We do our own thing. We put our stamp on all the work we do. The choice of material is ours, and nobody is going to tell us we can't do it."

A blessing of NPR's unusual structure is freedom from the contemporary media tyranny of "everyone's covering it, so we've got to, too." An interview with Weiss happened to come two days after Salt Lake City teenager Elizabeth Smart had been found in the company of her kidnappers, long after much of the country had given her up for dead. Weiss had just told her one reporter based in the interior West that this story was "not where I want you to spend your time." The very idea of such a thing would have given most producers hives. A story like this? They're all over it for days, each seeking to be louder and flashier than the other. Which is exactly why Weiss didn't want to be covering it. It was a big story, for sure. They had covered it for three program cycles. Now, Weiss wanted her reporter back on the piece he was working on before Smart was found: The tale of a town of some fifteen hundred people—forty-five of whom are about to leave for the National Guard. With talk building of war in Iraq, this was the kind of news Americans needed to be hearing, thought Weiss, who has the luxury of evaluating a story based not just on how fascinating it is, but "how it affects people's lives."

There's no editor around who's going to tell Weiss she must stay with the Smart story—and she thinks listeners won't, either. "If you assume people want the O. J. trial and that's all you give them, that's what they expect. We've been successful by giving them more." Weiss knows press-coverage orgies. She was executive producer of *ATC* for thirteen years—a period during which BOTH O. J. Simpson and Monica Lewinsky broke. "We obviously have a responsibility to tell the story. But to what degree do we have to tell it all the time, and let it crowd out other things?"

Then there's the opposite rut: the "nobody is covering it, so we'd better not cover it, either" pattern. That, too, tends to be shunned at NPR. "Every decision about what you put on the air is a value judgment," says Weiss. But this is a medium far less fearful than most about being "too out there," from early coverage of the bathhouses in the gay community as the AIDS crisis struck, to self-told tales of addiction.

Sixteen, 17, 18, 19—the whole time is like a fog. Shooting at people and getting shot at, hustling every waking moment, back and forth to jail. Love? That died with my mother.

Weiss says, "I kind of go back to the Constitution. I really feel like we have a very important role in the democratic process: To bring as much information as possible" to the citizens "so they can go out and make a decision. Not to give them only things they're comfortable with." And this—a rare sentiment in a world of hype: "I've done my job when I've taken something black and white and [listeners] say, 'Ah, it's gray.'"

In 1992, when the Supreme Court was hearing arguments over abortion restrictions that could have provided the occasion to overturn *Roe v. Wade,* Wertheimer reported one of those "gray" pieces. She interviewed four married women telling the stories of their decades-old illegal abortions. The pieces looked at the decisions that led up to their choice, the experience itself, the aftermaths. One had flown to Puerto Rico. One found a former nurse who performed the operation without anesthesia. One did the abortion herself. Another pursued her goal in the classic back-alley setting. Several wound up in the hospital. Two of these women eventually became opponents of abortion. Two ended up being supporters.

Reader responses poured in: "I never heard anybody really explain. . . . I've already believed . . . I thought I understood . . . ." As Weiss says, "This is about human beings. None of this is simple. Abortion has consequences that can last a lifetime. Consequences that might lead you to one side or might lead you to the other." Ah. It's gray.

Wertheimer is not given to indulging in emotionalism, but rather to statements like "I do NOT think that I'm supposed to make the world safe for democracy" and "I am not a subscriber to 'those were the good old days.'" And, "it's hard for me to see myself as trying to reveal the way, truth and light." Yet she recalls this story powerfully. "Four women in their fifties and sixties who were talking about experiences from their 'teens and twenties. Long conversations. Two of them felt what they had done was terrible. Two felt what they went through, no one should have to. Lots of people had no idea what not having abortion [as an option] was like. The essay gave them a powerful sense. It's not the sort of story you'd find elsewhere—except, maybe, a [newspaper's] Sunday magazine. Not on television, certainly. No one would allow something to go on at that length. Just one woman talking to another woman. The fear and sadness and anger."

All those shades of gray.

Wertheimer puts her finger on another singularity caused by NPR's unique structure. "We do not have the competition for the news hole." She's talking about space in the newspaper—an increasingly rare commodity in these profit-pressured days. But she's also talking about space on broadcast news shows. "At ABC, there's blood all over the floor about what gets in and what doesn't," she recalls a colleague telling her. "We have two hours every morning and two hours every evening. I would say there's just no question that you can get on the air with a good story. And you have breathing room to continue reporting."

To be sure, there are voices that caution that NPR is far less free of market pressures than it used to be. Interestingly, there was a "Business and Journalism Values" session at the annual Public Radio Conference in Washington in 2002. The *Columbia Journalism Review* covered it, noting "There is some concern that success might spoil NPR. As the stakes rise, says Dvorkin, programming tends to become risk averse. 'No one comes down to the news department and says, "Do more stories that are more accessible to a larger audience," but I think that we've become addicted to money. And that becomes a kind of self-censorship; we know at a subconscious level what's acceptable and what's not acceptable.'"

Dvorkin says that indeed he thinks financial pressures are daunting for public radio because listener support and financial support and foundation support "are all dependent on the health of the national economy." Though Dvorkin says he doesn't know of stories withheld out of such concerns, local station managers often feel pressure not to offend major donors. Some managers, he says, are "adept and sophisticated at handling this. Others find it an enormous challenge—but they also know that, to retreat into documentaries about hammered dulcimer players—yes, it serves an audience, but not as broad an audience as the news does."

In the end, despite the financial challenges, Dvorkin says NPR "still sees its audience as citizens—citizens first and listeners second. The thing that has impressed me so much is how this public service commitment is part of the mother's milk of this place." And then Dvorkin begins to read from Siemering.

It seems that, for most NPR staffers, the relative market freedom—in Wertheimer's words—continues to "foster a collegial atmosphere. The lack of commercial pressure makes a big difference. In theory, we should be able to make a heckuva lot of money. But that isn't the way we do it. We make decisions about things that are 'worth doing.' We are still sitting here talking about 'the right thing to do,' when so many organizations are imprisoned by the stock price.

"Where is it written that you have to have 22 percent of your profit returned?"

The Competition

When it comes to determining why NPR seems to shine so brightly these days, one other fact stands out: Everyone else is looking so bad, particularly when it comes to radio news. That's the point Ken Stern wants to make. Stern is executive vice president of NPR and looks the part. Call him Ellen Weiss's stylistic opposite. Stern is also the new guy, having joined NPR in 1999. Yale Law degree, Phi Beta Kappa, a success story who has done good as well as having done well.

"One of the reasons NPR has expanded is the abandonment by others of the core mission of producing in-depth news—in broadcast, and in particular, in radio," he says. Stern deplores the degree to which Clear Channel, which owns twelve hundred stations—most in major outlets—has changed the way radio is done. It "takes the majority of stations out of the news." Indeed, the founder and CEO of Clear Channel is a terrific guy to be up against, if you value radio news. Here's *Fortune* magazine's characterization in "Not the Bad Boys of Radio: Lowry Mays and sons made enemies building Clear Channel into an empire":

Lowry Mays is the Big Daddy of radio. The founder and CEO of Clear Channel, Mays oversees 1,233 radio stations with some 100 million listeners across all 50 states, and runs a company with $8 billion in revenues and a $23 billion market cap. But ask Mays about what he does for a living and you won't hear much about musicians or how to bring up ratings or who's the best DJ. Those things don't interest him much. Truth is, Mays isn't that passionate about what goes out over the airwaves. As long as his broadcasts sell ads, he's happy. "If anyone said we were in the radio business, it wouldn't be someone from our company," says Mays, 67. "We're not in the business of providing news and information. We're not in the business of providing well-researched music. We're simply in the business of selling our customers products."

(Clear Channel was sold to private equity firms for $19 billion in November 2006.)

No wonder Stern believes that, "In part, NPR has grown because others have vacated the field"—and not just in radio. He laments the "headline-focused, shout-focused world of supposed news programs on much of cable. It's increasingly hard to find careful, balanced, in-depth news. Broadcast doesn't do many stories. Even the twenty-four-hour networks take one or two stories a day, which they label breaking news and then pound the hell out of them. The story of NPR is a story of decisions made by others."

Jay Kernis—the NPR executive who left for *60 Minutes* and returned—notes that classic pieces on that much-admired news show had been fifteen minutes long. When he arrived they were thirteen and a half minutes. "When I left, it was eleven and a half, with more commercial space and more promotional space. Believe me, a lot is lost between thirteen and a half and eleven and a half. At NPR, if you have a good idea, there's a place for it. I can't say that was true at CBS. Also, I found that, for all the times that you try to break the boundaries, television still is very happy in the formula. All the time I was in television, I thought, 'God, NPR is so good. *Nightline* and *60 Minutes* come close. But most people in TV don't have the WILL to do this every day." Weiss says that when she came in 1982, "NPR had one person overseas—in London. Now it supports sixteen news bureaus and offices internationally." Meanwhile, other broadcast media have pretty much abandoned international news bureaus, she says.

NPR's growing strength in relation to other news media has an important component—one that some feel has made the network less special than it used to be. As Stern puts it: "If you looked back ten years, you could say that NPR was a much different place. It was a second-day story place. It could have charted a different path. But it took this one, and it has grown enormously over the past ten years." It has now become a primary source of information for most of its listeners—a change that many trace to the first Gulf War, which NPR sent its own reporters to cover. Since that change, says Weiss, "Our expectation of ourselves—and the expectation of our listeners—is that we're going to be there." Listening to a program from 2003, and then sampling shows from ten and twenty years ago, the observer can't help but be struck by the increase in foreign news, the quickened tempo, the—well, more "authoritative" voice. Even—dare we say it—a more "establishment" tone. No more Susan Stamberg asking listeners why April is the cruelest month.

In the spring of 1980 there were 237 NPR stations and 2,645,600 listeners, according to Arbitron figures. A decade later, 395 stations and 8,307,100 listeners. By 2005, there were more than 900 stations and well over 30 million listeners. The reach for—and the grasp of—a broader audience has changed the network, a change not without its cost, in Weiss's mind: "What worries me most is the growing demands. We fill so much air time now. I worry about, as we expand, we're giving people less time to do reporting. Trying to squeeze more out of people. We shouldn't sound just like everyone else."

At NPR—as in most organizations—the criticism and the concerns about change are a recurring theme. When *Morning Edition* launched in 1979—a more hard-news-focused program, with different pacing and different structure—loyalists lamented the passing of the old national hometown radio feel of NPR. In 1990, CJR commemorated NPR's twentieth anniversary with a piece headlined "Has Success Spoiled NPR?" The gist: Less Siemering's unique vision, more Washington establishment. Some loyalists inside agree. Says Weiss: "We became very risk-averse when we became successful. We became safe." Stern is unmoved. For all of his talk about more listeners, more donations, more resources to do more—and attract more listeners—he takes NPR out of the realm of the usual business spiel. "As a noncommercial public-service institution, we spend more time thinking about broadening our audience than our brethren in ways that may not make business sense."

NPR, he said, is eager to reach beyond its demographer's-dream listenership profile. For one thing, the average age is forty-nine. Many, like Weiss, wish "that we could figure out our next audience—give young people something." NPR seeks not only a younger but more ethnically diverse listenership—a goal that, despite Siemering's grand vision, has continued to be in large part unmet. The network has hired two new anchors for *ATC*—both relatively young, one African-American. And, with a group called the Public Radio African-American Consortium, it launched a new show with former BET network's Tavis Smiley. After three years, Smiley left the program saying NPR was not doing enough to reach minority listeners. NPR created a new program for that time slot with journalist Ed Gordon beginning in January 2005, and Fara Chideya replaced Gordon in September 2006.

One area of diversity NPR appears to have handled with more success is ideological diversity. For years, the network was the target of charges of liberal bias by organizations like the Heritage Foundation and Accuracy in Media. Liberals would in turn launch charges that the drift was turning rightward. In fact, the audience profile indicates that NPR listeners are close to reflecting the national political outlooks of American adults in general, though the percentage identifying themselves as liberal is modestly higher. Gingrich, whose opposition to NPR during his congressional leadership days sometimes seemed sufficient to kill the network, now says, "Either it is a lot less on the left, or I have mellowed." Indeed, NPR has found itself attacked from the other end of the spectrum as well. The liberal media-criticism group Fairness and Accuracy in Media contended in a 2004 study that both sources and commentators at NPR were considerably likelier to be conservative than liberal.

The main political charge heard these days, according to former ombudsman Dvorkin and to CPB reports to Congress, concerns Middle East coverage. Indeed, the experience of Boston's WBUR on this question illustrates just how tough being "listener-supported" can be. WBUR has lost 10 out of its 250 or so underwriters over the past three years—a hit that former WBUR spokeswoman Mary Stohn translated into a $1 million to $2 million loss, quite a chunk out of a $20 million annual budget. The losses stem from a boycott led by Boston-based CAMERA (Campaign for Accuracy in Middle East Reporting in America), which charges that WBUR (and NPR) coverage is consistently biased against Israel. WBUR has responded assertively, assigning staffers to listen to and investigate complaints, and meeting with CAMERA and other critics regularly—and also communicating frequently with NPR. As a consequence, says Dvorkin, "We made some changes in our journalistic procedures by reinforcing our own standards and practices with editors and reporters." NPR has also put its Mideast coverage transcripts on its Web site, "so listeners could double check what they heard against the written scripts. That has been effective in making our journalism more accountable and transparent," Dvorkin says.

WBUR's Stohn noted that such aggressive responses are essential because of a member station's direct reliance on its community. "I think that it's a lot easier if you are, say, the *New York Times*—not that the *Times* isn't going to review these things carefully. But their take is: 'Look, this is how we do our journalism, this is how the process works, it's not what you think—an agenda—it can't work that way, and here's why,' and then they can walk away. We're not in that position. We're depending upon the community and the goodwill of the community to keep us afloat. Unfortunately, we have to have our hand out because that's how we make our budget."

Dvorkin says he feels confident that such pressures will not result in a shying away from thorough coverage of the Middle East. Journalists can never be diligent enough about fairness, he says, but even fairness achieved would be "difficult for people who are partisans—who want informational comfort food, and can get that from other media." There was, in 2003, said Dvorkin, "a kind of patriotic anxiety. People want to be comforted. We will comfort them, but that's not all we should do."

Siemering would say that the network's commitment to ideological balance came, from the start, with an emphasis on strong journalistic credentials. But if ideological charges have a harder time sticking these days, the question of whether NPR is more conventional and less innovative than it used to be has more staying power. Consider the question of David Giovannoni. His Audience Research Analysis of public radio's audience is perhaps the main reason NPR now reaches so many more people than it used to, and a primary reason why NPR is so much more self-sufficient financially. Thanks in large part to Giovannoni, NPR pays more attention to what the audience likes and wants than it used to—a fact that some would say is the primary threat to NPR's singularity. He's been called a "numbers Nazi" whose compelling audience research has caused NPR to make "a deal with the devil."

Yet, for those accustomed to the cold reality of most media CEO decisions today, Giovannoni sounds downright soulful. He is given to quoting Siemering and the Core Values, and to talking about taking risks, "budgeting to fail if necessary" and "the business of public service." Nonetheless, a *Washington Monthly* piece chided NPR for increasing homogeneity of programming and voice, adding: "It's frightening to imagine what NPR will sound like a decade from now—lots of stories about colonoscopies and

Rod Stewart still going strong at 65." On the other hand, the efforts NPR does set forth to bring about change risk offending its loyal listener base— as became clear when the clumsy demotion of *Morning Edition* host Bob Edwards in 2004 sparked an e-mail protest some thirty-five thousand strong.

Still, for the most part, happiness reigns at NPR. In interview after interview, this open and eager staff—even those raising concerns—called their own employer "a national treasure" and spoke of the "incredible honor and privilege" of working there. Not a common song among journalists these days.

Meanwhile, NPR's influence spreads. Says Dan Schorr: "When I left CNN in 1985, and NPR asked me if I wanted to do some commentaries for them, my attitude was, 'Oh, what the hell, I may as well. No one will ever know what I'm doing.' I thought of it as semi-retirement. I didn't realize that NPR today is major media in terms of the size of its audience, in terms of its influence." *Morning Edition* and *All Things Considered* each draw larger weekly audiences than any individual evening news broadcast. NPR's twenty-six million weekly audience exceeds the combined circulation of the top forty-two daily newspapers in the United States.

And listeners love it. At the end of the broadcast that so compelled me during that rainy March afternoon drive to the airport, listeners across the nation were feeling powerfully moved: "Blak's tale was riveting. It was beautiful to hear Yanier Moore's mortal struggle to maintain a glimmer of hope and to find dignity and meaning in the midst of all that life could heap upon him. There were moments I found it difficult to drive when tears blurred the street. It took a while before I wanted to break the spell and return to my world." Others wrote of having been distracted from impending war, for the first time in many days. Or indeed, of having been reminded that we have in our own country, scenes as awful as war. Deborah Warshaw, a teacher in rural Colorado, said that Moore's "beautifully written and recorded story" had reminded her why she does what she does, for "this is why what happens in the classroom is important. Some anonymous person in some school helped this person survive by helping him see why reading and writing matters."

And that flicker of hope? It was like a little birthday candle in like a tornado. But now it's like a bonfire. I got high hopes now. If I was to go penniless tomorrow or today, my book would still be there for them to say, "My daddy did something!" They can't say, "My daddy never did anything but sell drugs or gang bang." Now they can say, "My daddy had a book out. He did something."

Blak, the newly published author whose work was celebrated that day, talked about how he thinks NPR is different from CNN or the *New York Times,* the local newspaper or TV station:

> Because it actually touches people as kind of real. After doing this piece, people started contacting me from all walks of life. A middle school teacher in Oklahoma told me, "Wow! The life I live is nothing like that. I only worry about picking the kids up from the sitter on time. Listening to you just really gave me an uplifting moment." I didn't understand the power of NPR until actually doing this piece and then getting the response from it. Other media, they just pick and choose what they think is newsworthy—usually something sensational, some corrupt politician or baby missing. NPR is kind of giving a voice to people and things you never hear. It gives you kind of an insight. It actually shows you a part of America—of our world—that people don't know really exists, cause they're getting all their information so air-brushed and touched-up and made to look this way or that. NPR is more of a raw image. It's just more real.

Bill Siemering's January 2003 "manifesto," "My First Fifty Years in Radio and What I Learned," quotes Abraham Lincoln: 'Let the people know the facts and the country will be safe.' I am a firm believer in the people. If given the truth, they can be depended upon to meet any crisis. The great point is to bring them the real facts." Siemering himself notes that "freedom of the press by itself is no guarantee that the interests of democracy will be served. Media must be independent and responsible. If they aren't responsible, they undermine civil society." Siemering is in large part responsible for NPR and for its determination NOT to undermine, but rather to nourish. Thirty years and many millions of listeners later, when Siemering talks about National Public Radio, his voice is warm with pride and hopefulness.

Sources

The content of this chapter comes from interviews in the winter and spring of 2003. These include in-person sessions at National Public Radio's Washington headquarters with NPR employees Jeffrey Dvorkin, Susan Stamberg, Linda Wertheimer, Jay Kernis, Ellen Weiss, and Ken Stern, who became chief executive officer in 2006. I also conducted telephone interviews with NPR employees Robert Siegel, Marcus Rosenbaum, and Daniel Schorr, and with former

NPR employees William Buzenberg and Bill Siemering. Also included are telephone and e-mail conversations with listeners who had written letters to NPR, and with "Blak" and with Mary Stohn of WBUR in Boston.

Other sources, in print and online:

A paper written in the fall of 1986, "Some Things to Consider about Audience Building," by Bill Siemering, was sent to me by Siemering, as was "My First Fifty Years in Radio and What I Learned." "The Business of Public Service" by David Giovannoni, from the ARAnet online library of Public Radio Research, was originally published as a keynote address July 11, 2001.

"All Things Considerate: How NPR Makes Tavis Smiley Sound like Linda Wertheimer," by Brian Montopoli, *Washington Monthly,* January/February 2003.

"National Prosperous Radio," *Time,* March 24, 2003.

"Public Radio: Firewalls and Funding," by Judith Hepburn Blank, *Columbia Journalism Review,* May 2005.

"NPR losing War of Words on Mideast Coverage," by Mark Jurkowitz, *Boston Globe,* January 15, 2003.

Online

www.npr.org.

www.wbur.org.

www.prpd.org (the public radio programmers' association, on Defining Core Values).

www.aranet.com.

www.camera.org (Campaign for Accuracy in Middle East Reporting in America).

The Hometown Newspaper Builds Community

The journalism that matters most to most Americans is local. Even in this electronic era, the local newspaper is the foundation of serious journalism. With staffs far larger than those of television or radio, and with a commitment to serving the best interests of their communities, newspapers such as the Anniston Star *stand at the heart of cities and towns across America. The history of the* Star *shows that a courageous newspaper can prosper and help its community to prosper and grow. The author, Judy Bolch, a native of the South, spent most of her career at the* News & Observer *in Raleigh, North Carolina, where she eventually became managing editor. Now she holds the Harte Chair in Innovation at the Missouri School of Journalism.*

The words on the editorial page that August day were blunt and heartbreaking:

> We have had our generals and our gallant heroes. Now we have our Willie Brewster.
>
> We have had our scientists, our statesmen, our men of industry and commerce. Now we have our Willie Brewster.
>
> We have built our schools and churches. We have extolled our past and sung glad songs of our future.
>
> And we have made a society which produced the murderer of Willie Brewster.

Willie Brewster: Foundry worker. Gardener. Husband. Father. *Black.* Shot dead by a racist after a minister led a rally on the courthouse steps, exhorting his listeners to kill if that was what it took to get black men off white men's streets.

That 1965 editorial ran in the *Anniston Star,* an Alabama paper whose owner three days earlier had helped find three hundred people to pledge twenty thousand dollars to anyone who could identify the killer and, perhaps more important in those violent days, to condemn such acts by publishing their names in the paper. Not objective journalism? That editor has no apologies. "Who can be 'objective' about a racial murder or the denial of basic American rights?" he asks today.

Fast-forward three decades to the mid-nineties. A delegation of blacks, practically the community's "entire civil rights roundtable," storms the same owner's office. Many are now part of the town's power structure. They're incensed at the paper's reporting that anti-poverty money bought a Lincoln stretch limo for an agency headed by the very civil rights veteran once beaten when he tried to integrate the public library. In the meeting, "racism" is a word heard frequently.

Which pieces are "good" community journalism? Does either—or both—illustrate what a "good" newspaper writes in its pages? It all depends on whom you ask and *when* you ask them. The same contingent, indeed some of the same people, who praised the *Star'*s liberal stances in the sixties was now calling it racist for applying color-blind standards.

But the real criterion isn't merely what the readers think. Judge a newspaper by the long-term role it plays in its community, a role that often seems to bounce back and forth from leader to cheerleader, a role integral to what the community itself becomes. Judge a newspaper by the fact that even though there are those who love it and those who hate it, there is no one who imagines that the city would be the same had the newspaper never existed.

This is the town. Anniston, Alabama. A town, after all, is the "community" in community journalism. This is a town where "honeys" and "darlings" addressed to strangers blossom like the mimosa and magnolia trees; where religious stations dominate the talk radio dial and Trucker Tom gets a host's "manly man" verdict on the sixteen-wheeler horn blown for listeners' edification. Where until 2002, the names of the local "colored" and white World War I casualties were segregated on a stone monument and where now a white college boy dining on the veranda of the town's ritziest hotel rises to introduce a black friend to his date. Where a third generation still runs the family-owned newspaper.

This is a town born of a couple of nineteenth-century capitalists who wanted to keep their iron foundry workers happy. They planted one hundred thousand water oaks in an orderly grid. They built cottages, churches, schools, a mill, a dairy, a store, a theater, and everything a fenced-in population could need. They gave workers equity in their houses—creating citizens instead of indentured servants. They paid them up to a dollar a day, when others paid a maximum sixty cents. They installed electric lights. Their enterprise was altruistic. It was visionary. It was profitable. At first, they called the place Woodstock after the iron company. Then they named it Anniston—Annie's Town—christened, legend has it, after one founder's daughter. Annie's town had a newspaper, too: the *Hot Blast,* so-called because of the furnace. The *Hot Blast,* owned by the company, lived up to its namesake, promoting its causes with fire, outwitting and outlasting the dozens of other newspapers that came and went, keeping the owners' political influence strong even as the fence came down to admit outsiders.

Grace Gates, a local historian, wrote that Anniston was a "model city of the New South." It won national recognition for being "special." But controversy, Gates said, was "almost always the underlying current." The controversies would include those many Alabama towns faced: race, poverty, a fierce determination to maintain identity without sinking with the ship of Southernness. Anniston today reflects the lingering effects of that past. For it, the New South, that powerful promise of reconciliation and imported economic ingenuity, has come and gone or never existed, depending on who's asked. Yet the model city's vision—"We are different because we believe we are"—persists.

Once, twenty-some years ago, a local reporter wrote about Anniston's struggle "to find its secret—its underlying theme—and give it a name. If the theme can be so defined, I think it is this: That change in the city is like a current over jagged bedrock. It flows, slowly or quickly, and as it does it wears down the rock of 'was,' of the past; but the rock lasts a long time, and directs the current's flow toward 'will be.'"

The town's newspaper has always helped direct that current, sometimes gently, sometimes urgently, pushing the water forward, trying to smooth the jagged edges without marring the bedrock. Soon, the newspaper's own life will take a new direction, one, however, still intricately intertwined with the fate of the place its owners have served for more than one hundred years.

This is the news. There's a picture in the July 6, 2003, *New York Times Magazine.* It shows Darline Stephens of Anniston, Alabama, standing stiffly, arms behind back. She wears a bold plaid shirt. She also wears a flimsy plastic hood attached in some unseen way to a strange contraption on her chest. A massive tag hangs from the contraption, which turns out to be a charcoal filter. "SCAPEhood," reads the tag. The picture, one in the magazine's "What They Were Thinking" series, has this caption: "I live about 5 or 10 miles from chemical weapons. We're over there searching for weapons of mass destruction in Iraq, but we have them here in our hometown."

This picture is exactly why some Annistonians love—and hate—The *Star.* First, a bit of background on the reason an ordinary woman from small-town America is modeling a hood; on why she and some twenty-three thousand others, including babies, have been issued this $225 bit of shabby-looking protection; on why they worry about terrorist attacks and leaks and government-mandated burnings that could disperse nerve agents or mustard gas or other chemical weapons into the air or onto the earth. No matter what color alert the nation recognizes from day to day, these people are always in the pink zone, the area nearest the Anniston Army Depot. There wait more than half a million deteriorating rockets, mortars, projectiles, and mines armed with the deadly chemicals: twenty-two hundred tons of them, 7 percent of the nation's supply and its biggest single stockpile. The weapons were shipped to Anniston in the 1960s to be stored in case of war. Now international treaty binds the United States to destroy all chemical weapons by 2007. The government built a $1 billion incinerator to do the job for Anniston. But some of the hundreds of thousands of people in the nearby counties believed fumes from the incinerator itself would pose serious danger. They wanted the weapons "disassembled, neutralized and secondarily treated," according to a lawsuit filed by public interest, environmental, and religious groups. Shortly after the *New York Times* picture appears, the incineration—the approach pushed by the *Star* after long investigation—begins.

Like all papers determined to give its community the facts necessary for informed opinion, the *Star* has never let up on the issue. The *Star* wouldn't take a stand on the chemicals until it met with scientists from the National Academy of Science. It sent an editor to Johnston Island, an atoll about seven hundred miles from Honolulu, to stand right at the door of the incinerator where similar chemicals were being destroyed. That was one way to prove its belief in the safety of incineration. In early 2003, the *Star* published an ambitious five-part series called "A Matter of Trust." Written by a reporter who traveled to Hermiston, Oregon, to see why that community was better prepared to deal with its stockpile, the series attempted to sort Anniston facts from fears.

Therein lies the rub, or perhaps the stink. What the *Star* writes about, national media outlets take note of. The paper's national reputation assures it. For Mayor Hoyt W. (Chip) Howell and other community leaders trying to promote Anniston, that is not an unmixed blessing. Asked about the paper's relationship with the community, Howell pauses. CNN has been in town today covering the incinerator story. NBC's *Nightly News* was there last week. They are just the latest in a long line of national reporters descending. Howell is more than a bit tired of it all. The attitude toward the paper, he says finally, "varies from day to day. Certainly its position has always been to represent those not having another voice. They've been very consistent with that." With the PCB situation, for example, he says, the *Star* was right there: "identifying the problem, informing the public of the impact and bringing it to a head as soon as possible."

The PCBs, fallout from a Monsanto plant that produced the chemicals from 1929 to 1971, pollute land and water. The federal government finally funded a $3.2 million study on how the PCBs (polychlorinated biphenyls, used, in this case, mostly for electrical equipment) have affected residents. The mayor knows and appreciates that such news needs to be told. "But occasionally the community gets a little angry with someone exposing the warts that may develop in an environmental or political discord," he says. "You're never happy with bad news. They report things the way they see them. Facts are facts, and it's up to the reader to interpret. They're biased on occasion, but for the most part factual." But he hates labels like "Toxic Town USA" and "America's worst place to live" that the national media have thrust upon Anniston. "The *Star* has been very visible in the current crises. They've been a supporter as we move through the process. But there's resentment that we wouldn't be getting the national attention had the *Star* not been so flagrant in its reporting." No matter what successes the *Star* later reports, he claims, bad national publicity won't be reversed. The big media don't arrive en masse for the good news.

Donald W. Stewart, lawyer for the plaintiffs in the state case against Monsanto et al., acknowledges that the *Star*'s reporters did a good job covering the PCB problem. But, says Stewart, whose clients will share part of a recent $700 million settlement, the editorial-page staff "missed the boat." *Star* owner/publisher H. Brandt Ayers, he claims, "chose not to take a stand for the community." Stewart thinks it took the *Star* longer than it should have to acknowledge PCB health hazards.

Chris Waddle, a long-time editor at the *Star*, says the paper's initial editorial stance was handicapped by the uncertain state of scientific research.

Besides, he adds, the paper always took the position that the PCBs had to be cleaned up. And . . . um . . . he adds, Stewart may also be a bit miffed because he lost a $20 million libel suit against the paper. Then there were those unflattering stories when Stewart was running for the U.S. Senate.

"A paper is not known by its friends but by its independence and willingness to go where the story is," says Waddle. Somehow a lot of the paper's friends seem to make the news. "We marvel that so many of our friends get burned," he says. "We wish it didn't happen, but let the chips fall where they may."

Some *Star* editors were too much in favor of incineration, says Pete Conroy, and he believes that bias led the paper to downplay alternative technologies for destruction of the chemical weapons. But Conroy, director of the Environmental Policy and Information Center at nearby Jacksonville State University, gives the paper an A overall for environmental coverage. "I couldn't be more complimentary about a newspaper anywhere in the country," says Conroy, who has been in the area for some twenty years. "The issues are so complicated, it's hard to get the grass down where the goats can eat it." He thinks the *Star*'s "superlative" and "extraordinary" reporting has kept the public informed at the cost of sometimes infuriating community leaders and advertisers.

This is the paper that makes a difference. The St. Louis publisher who declared newspapers to be either thermometers (which take the temperature) or thermostats (which take action) would know where the *Star* fits. Twice, *Time* magazine has named it one of the nation's best small papers. *Columbia Journalism Review* listed it among the top thirty-five papers, regardless of size. The American Society of Newspaper Editors awarded Ayers its 2003 Award for Editorial Leadership. All mighty nice, of course, but just what IS it about the *Star*?

Examine only a few editions, and its power isn't obvious. It seems pretty much like any well-designed, well-written small paper. Take a closer look. Read the paper for a while, and you'll find the answer: passion for place. The *Star*'s stories unfold like chapters of a book, day after day, making the connections between past and present. The *Star* offers a continuing story, not one of unconnected information. The *Star*'s news sections tell us; its editorial pages motivate us. One feature of its Web site—Issues—documents its commitment to follow-through. There, the most casual viewer can find the news that breaks in tiny meaningless pieces now pulled together, creating continuity out of the chaos of daily newspapering. As Ayers once wrote, the story that needs to be told is of "the whole amazing pageant of southern history—the saga of migration from continent to continent and from farm to city, of wars waged and lost, of atrocities committed and borne, of loving and hating, of the long trek from poverty to better times—a journey that blacks and whites took together."

Through the years, the *Star* has helped lead change after change. The paper, for example, discovered that city officials were awarding business on the basis of friendship rather than on sealed bids. Officials were also "buying" more janitorial supplies for one building than most cities did for their entire operations. A telescopic shot showed the mayor's bagman reaching into the post office box where the checks for those supplies were being sent. Citizens rose up, threw out the officials, and voted in a new city-manager form of government. When the *Star* found that the jury list, which just happened to include the names of convicted felons, was being compiled by the publisher of a racist hate sheet, it led the drive for a new jury selection process.

In Anniston, the paper's influence, like the one-hundred-plus-degree heat, is a given.

Wander around the downtown where the beauty of late nineteenth- and early twentieth-century architectural history is slowly being reborn. Marvel at the Calhoun County Courthouse, just one of the buildings whose deep, dark, alluring red bricks seem to shout the town's red-clay origins. Admire Zinn Park, an oasis of rich green landscape edged by the old black section. There the First Baptist Church is for sale. Some of the houses have been reclaimed, but many are peeling with poverty. Half of Anniston's twenty-four thousand residents are white; half are black. Almost half the households earn less than twenty-five thousand dollars a year. The city schools are almost totally black, the middle classes of both races having left the system. Where once cast-iron pipe, chemicals, and textiles were the dominant industries, the metro area now is a regional center for banking, medicine, and retail. Its major employer is Anniston Army Depot, where forty-seven hundred employees refit tanks and missiles and build the Army's new Stryker combat vehicle. Nearby, a giant Honda plant is still growing.

Drop in at the King's Palace, really just an old-fashioned barbershop complete with striped pole. It's owned by Yong Orlowski, a Korean who moved here with her soldier husband. The white-haired man she's styling is Donald H. Curry, a longtime member of the board of education and the county commission. At seventy-two and a half years of age, he's had a *Star* subscription ever since he learned to pick out the words in the headlines. He doesn't always agree with its stances but thinks the paper pretty much reflects the community. "Ninety-nine percent of the time, it's on target," he says.

Drive over to Wendy's on Quintard Avenue and ask the high school student serving up fries how she feels about the *Star.* Yes, she gets it at home. Yes, she likes to read about sports and the honor roll and "what's going on in the world."

Stop by the world-class Calhoun County Chamber of Commerce building a bit farther along tree-lined Quintard. "People here read the *Star* every day and talk about it, " says chamber president Sherri J. Sumners. "I'm never far into the day before someone mentions something. It really does set the stage for all conversations. Brandy's column is a must-read, particularly when you don't agree with him."

Attention, it seems, must be paid.

All words to make an editor dance in the streets. All nice but not terribly surprising for an almost twenty-seven-thousand-circulation paper that circulates in several counties but whose home is a town of just twenty-four thousand. Here's what *is* surprising. Listen to how Cleophus Thomas, Jr., a leading attorney rumored in line to become Alabama's first black governor, puts it: "The *Star* is a dominant player in its field—in the big leagues and right at home. Brandy is a nationally recognized columnist and commentator. People are aware he's a national figure. The paper is like a looming natural presence. Like the Choccolocco Mountains, it's a force of nature."

To understand that presence, it's vital to return to the *Hot Blast,* the weekly that quickly turned into the *Daily Hot Blast.* That's where it all began for the Ayers family. Consider, thanks to historian Gates, the chronology of events: Daniel Tyler (a Union general and Connecticut capitalist) met Samuel Noble (a native Englishman and Confederate munitions manufacturer from Georgia). In 1872 they begat the Woodstock Iron Company that begat the model city Anniston that begat national attention. The *New York Herald* called it "the magic city." In 1883, the Georgia Pacific Railroad's westward push from Atlanta to Birmingham begat the need to run the rails through Anniston. That begat the need to open the town to the public, and, of course, to establish a company newspaper to tell all about it.

Then things get even more complicated. Suffice it to say that Brandy's grandfather Dr. T. W. Ayers bought a newspaper in Anniston. By the late nineteenth century, Ayers had also bought the *Daily Hot Blast,* where his first order of business was to push for good roads and fair freight rates. Liberalism—as defined by the belief that the status quo can always be status better—was the Ayers stamp. His journalism was more moderate than liberal in many cases, yet liberal in the context of time and place.

Like the son and grandson who would follow, Dr. Ayers was a man of passion. Three passions, in fact: newspapers, medicine, and religion. As historian Kevin Stoker documents, by 1901 Ayers had sold both newspapers and taken off for China as a Baptist missionary. He was forty-one years old, and four of his six children, including Brandy's father, went along. The sight of cotton goods from Anniston being sold in Hwang-hsieu amazed young Harry Mell Ayers, then fifteen. "And the longer I stayed there, watching the impact of Western culture on the Chinese mind, the more I became impressed with the inescapable solidarity of mankind—the fact that no nation can live for itself alone," he wrote later.

Three years later, Harry was back in Anniston, working for the *Daily Hot Blast* for six dollars a week. By 1906, he was at the *Anniston Evening Star.* By 1910, he had bought the *Daily Hot Blast* and by 1912 had, in conjunction with a close friend whose winning campaign for governor he ran, consolidated it with the *Evening Star.* The new venture became the *Anniston Star.* And Harry—later known as "Colonel," an honorary post in the Alabama National Guard—was quickly on his way to making the nation sit up and take notice.

Not that the Colonel ever wrote for national publications. But he was adept at making his journalistic friends, many from great old Southern newspaper families like the Daniels of North Carolina and the Binghams of Kentucky, aware of his editorials. Those pieces were reprinted everywhere. Colonel Ayers drew attention for his speeches and radio talks, too, and for his vigorous campaigning for liberal candidates. *Time* magazine quoted his speech advising "Yankee Youth" to come to the South for real opportunity. The speech was read into the *Congressional Record.* The *Star* published it as a pamphlet and sent it out to Southern papers. The Colonel would go on to become a delegate to the 1928 Democratic National Convention and later to visit Franklin D. Roosevelt and somewhat presumptuously announce: "I want the *Star* to be the first paper in the South to endorse you."

The Colonel had the instincts not just of a great newspaperman but also of a public-relations impresario. "Harry Ayers imbued the *Star* with a culture of national ambition and local tradition. He was also a smart businessman who liked to keep the *Star* in front of the community in the way it thought and the way it operated," says Stoker, an assistant professor at Brigham Young University, in an interview. "What made the *Anniston Star* effective under Harry Ayers was that it had an opinion, it had a soul, and it stood by through subscription cancellations and political disasters. That's the paradox of journalism. The great newspapers stand for something, while at the same time providing balanced news coverage." The Colonel's tocsin still rings at the top of the *Star*'s editorial page: "It is the duty of a news-paper to become the attorney for the most defenseless among its sub-scribers."

And soon the history of the *Star* will have an entirely new chapter, one that Harry Ayers, champion of education, would enthusiastically support.

This is the black and white. Alabama is haunted by the Scottsboro boys, by the four little girls who died in a church bombing, by Bull Connor, by so many vestiges of a tragic past. One knows racial issues still burn through-out the rest of America. One knows every state has its evils. Yet a visitor to Alabama hears the echoes, looks for the realities. When in the Birmingham airport a rental-car employee jumps into his personal car to ferry a traveler and her heavy luggage to the departure lounge, she's astounded by his Southern hospitality. He's a white man, retirement age, a veteran of pre–civil rights. Sitting in the back seat is a black woman. The man gestures, introduces her. "She's my . . . " He stops. " . . . We have a lot of fun to-gether," he finishes. The visitor is astounded again. The man hasn't come to terms with having a black friend he clearly values.

Anniston's past, too, is marked on the civil rights timeline. On Mother's Day, May 14, 1961, a Greyhound bus carrying Freedom Riders was fire-bombed just after leaving the town, sending some passengers to the hospi-tal and putting one Freedom Rider permanently in a wheelchair. An hour after the Greyhound, a Trailways bus carrying more Freedom Riders pulled into Anniston, and its passengers, too, were attacked. Law enforcement seems to have done little to help. On Mother's Day, May 12, 1963, white men shot into a black church and the homes of two black families. A few city leaders decided it was time to act, to form a biracial committee that could help defuse the tensions and, perhaps, just perhaps, lead the com-munity toward integration. Wilfred Gailbraith, then executive editor of the *Star,* agreed to serve on the new, possibly dangerous, Human Relations Council.

"There is little doubt that Wilfred felt real tension between his role as editor of the free press newspaper, whose job was to keep the community informed of issues and situations that affected the community, and his be-ing a member of the Council," writes the council's first chairman, Phil Noble, in a 2003 book, *Beyond the Burning Bus: The Civil Rights Revolution in a Southern Town.* Noble, then a Presbyterian minister in Anniston, was a white man who believed in equality for all. "The nature of what was happening and the ever-present possibility of violence required that much of the Council's work be behind the scenes activity which would serve the community best if it were not publicized in the newspaper. Wilfred basically respected the need for careful discrimination of what should be reported about the Council's work. I think he felt as journalists do in times of war or other extreme crisis when the press to some extent censors itself for the good of the country or the community. There's no doubt that we were locally engaged in a sort of war."

But unlike many Southern newspapers of that era, the *Star* covered and prominently displayed most of the civil rights battles. It wrote editorials at almost every turning point. The *Star* did not hesitate to condemn the violence nor to praise the council's work in convincing businessmen to take down the "colored" and "white" signs above water fountains and on public toilets. The council thought it was making progress. Yet on September 15, 1963, on the very same Sunday the little girls died in Birmingham, two "Negro" ministers were beaten as they tried to integrate the Anniston Public Library. The *Star* voice was heard on that dismaying day as well. And then in 1965 came the Willie Brewster murder, in which the efforts of the *Star* to find his killer shone so brightly.

In the seventies, *Star* leadership would again find itself in a leadership role that didn't often show up on the printed page. When the community found itself once more faced with racial unrest, Ayers was part of a backstage committee that quietly pushed to hire black police and black school principals. The committee was an action group, he says, but also a "place where things could be vetted and understanding could take place." In this case, he felt, reporting little on the group was the better part of wisdom.

By the mid-nineties when the delegation showed up in Ayers's office to protest the alleged "racism" in the limo piece, the mood was different. Blacks wanted Waddle, who initially revealed the situation in an editorial, to be fired. Waddle's editorial would spark a nineteen-month state and local investigation of the anti-poverty agency. That investigation uncovered bookkeeping chaos, hundreds of thousands of dollars of debt—and a very slow effort to find a buyer for the limo. Eventually, the Reverend N. Q. Reynolds, long one of Anniston's most prominent civil rights leaders and one of the two men injured in the initial attempt to integrate the library, was ousted as head of the agency. The agency itself was dissolved; a new body assumed some of its efforts to help the poor with rent, heat, and other needs. And by then the *Star* had further infuriated the black community with its stories on a councilwoman who hadn't repaid a city loan she took out to finance her dress shop.

It is difficult, looking back when so much has changed and so much has not, to evaluate the role of the Southern editors acclaimed for liberalism on rights for the common man. Most, like the Colonel, were men who pushed for reform, but who, trapped in the moment, did not really believe in a goal most now take for granted: social equality. Ayers says his father, who "led the fight to get equal pay for black teachers" and fought many other such battles, simply felt integration would be too disruptive. Equal—but still separate, says Ayers about his father's beliefs. One scholar notes that these country editors, as he calls them, liked the idea of the New South but couldn't quite break from the Old South role of the white man. And in their very Southernness, many reflected the sentiment that some things are best left unsaid. When a New York book editor visited Anniston in 1963, he was royally entertained by, among others, Ayers's sister, Elise. The editor returned to New York and published an article in *Mademoiselle* magazine that set Anniston, then a bigger town of some thirty-five thousand residents, ablaze. He mentioned the liquor store with a checkout counter divided by a fence, one side marked "white," one side "colored." He called the Colonel a "marvelous man" but one too old to change. He claimed "Nothing is happening" was the battle cry of the South, that ignoring the revolution was the weapon of choice. He wrote that Anniston's elite politely resisted his urgings about the need "to do something," then, on one occasion, exploded. They said, he wrote, that they hated Negroes, were afraid of them. They called them "disgusting, backward animals." The editor admitted to a sneaky feeling that all smart Southerners had departed the region, leaving behind only the stupid ones. A few months later, an Anniston author replied in *Mademoiselle,* denying these assessments, saying the outburst had not really happened, that the South knew change was inevitable, that the article was another by a Northerner determined to see what he wanted to see. At this late date, the facts about the events are unreachable, but, whoever is right, the exchange itself says much. In the Southern code, then as now, it is a sin to scratch the veneer of cordiality even when the most serious issues are involved.

And William B. McClain, the minister who, despite being violently rebuffed on his first try, returned the next day to integrate the Anniston Public Library, hints at such a continuing divide. Recently he noted with a touch of bitterness that the white people of the town and the *Anniston Star* itself still refer to the failed attempt as "The Incident at the Library." "That is not the way black people remember it," he says in Noble's book.

Many of Anniston's longtime black leaders evaluate the *Star* as having done an acceptable job covering civil rights. Some sympathize with the difficulty for a white paper, even with the best of wills, to truly understand the black viewpoint. They praise the Colonel and his son for their stances in the face of community opposition. Others are critical. "Back in the sixties," says the Reverend Roosevelt Parker, "the *Star* took the lead bringing people together and trying to solve racial problems. Now it's more of a dictator than a paper relating the feelings of African-Americans and other minorities." A former NAACP president, the reverend had canceled his subscription but is now subscribing because his wife wants the paper. He criticizes the *Star* for allegedly minimizing stories on his race's good achievements and on not strongly stressing the need to solve the black community's drug problems. Ignoring the latter, he says, violates the paper's oath to defend the underdog. "If you ask the black community, they think the *Star* as a whole is not helping the black community. Colonel Ayers did a better job. Brandy did a good job in the eighties, but leading into the nineties, his work went downhill." And in another of those cases where every new comment carries the weight of past connections, the Reverend Roosevelt says he is still irritated by a personal incident in which he and Ayers disagreed over who should chair a committee in Ayers's absence.

Ayers, buffered by the miles of newsprint he's expended in favor of civil rights and the years he's spent in the community working for progress, would, of course, rebut the reverend's stance. But he would, no doubt, understand it. As he wrote in a recent column, "In the South, blacks and whites have been locked together in a well-remembered history of hurting, being hurt, of atrocities committed and borne—and, always, above and beneath all else, an experience of caring."

Caring has always been the *Star*'s underlying foundation. Yet the saddest of codicils exists for the Colonel's fifty-four-year tenure at the *Star*. In 1956, the Colonel, then seventy, appeared on an American Society of Newspaper Editors panel discussing integration. Possibly suffering from a series of little strokes, the Colonel suddenly launched a confusing tirade that mixed quotations and his own views. He called blacks in general "dirty, shiftless cheats" and claimed that "the consuming desire of every Negro is to possess a young white woman." The Colonel would continue to run the *Star*, but his declining health became more and more of a problem; his editorials made less and less sense. By 1963, his son had been recalled from Washington, D.C., where he was working for a news bureau serving Southern papers. The son's duty, wrote Stoker, was a hateful one—to surreptitiously censor the Colonel's editorials.

The Colonel died on October 4, 1964, honored by his friends—black and white.

This is the publisher. It's 8 a.m. and Brandy Ayers is in his office a few days after returning from a London media conference. He's at his desk, dressed right sharp for one inhabiting the often-crumpled world of journalism. He wears a striped blue-and-white shirt with white collar and cuffs, a gold collar pin, and a red tie dotted with blue stars. The standard blue blazer hangs on a nearby chair. Despite his dash and the stylized purple suede chairs facing his desk, Brandy (everyone calls him that) inspires thoughts of an English country squire. He has the pointy features and steely gaze of a man who is both kind and determined.

His office occupies one of the pagoda-like "pods" dotting the *Star*'s third home, a $16 million facility, built in 2002 on twenty-two acres of decommissioned Fort McClellan. Inspired by the hilly landscape and by Anniston's industrial history, the architect created a sprawling design featuring native stone and wood, with hints of factory heritage in large windows and tin roof. The site lies near the middle of the city's new limits, doubled when the former fort was annexed. Most have forgiven the *Star* for moving beyond downtown, acknowledging its strenuous but unsuccessful efforts to find a suitable site there. But, as a painter at the Sherwin-Williams store notes, there's still dissatisfaction with the project's outside architect, contractors, builders, and carpenters. Why, he asks, weren't all locals selected? The *Star* ran letters to the editor voicing the same criticism. That kind of query is perhaps predictable in a town when everyone knows everyone else's business. But, as Ayers remembers it, using all locals would have added a million dollars to project cost.

This morning Ayers catches up on phone messages such as one from the woman whose child has a 160 IQ. She's asking about MENSA, the club for genius-level types. "She's sure that you are a member," Ayers's secretary tells him." "I got them fooled!" he interjects quickly. Then there are the e-mails, which he accesses with infinitely amateur keyboarding. An editorial cartoon about the Christian Coalition's non-Christian opposition to the governor's tax plan for the poor has elicited a firestorm. "The Christian Coalition is after me," Ayers announces. "Whoa!" E-mails are pouring in, claiming slan-

One thing that hasn't changed is Brandy Ayers. Wry wit. Courtly. Pure Southern when it suits him, urbane when that's a better fit. A writer whose rhythmic words leave their traces in the ears as well as in the mind. A liberal in most senses. "But," says Heath, "Brandy's detractors say he doesn't pay enough attention to the paper. That the paper is just his calling card for the big cheese stuff. They say at home he needs to be more focused on the paper and the region, that he's worried about starving children in Africa when we've got starving children in Alabama. It's that limousine liberal kind of thing."

This is the family. It's dinnertime at No. 1 Booger Hollow. Brandy and his wife join a guest for a drink in the study, home to his "Clinton Shrine." Theirs seems to be an unusually equitable partnership, each almost equally passionate and knowledgeable about the traditions that have brought them here. Josie Ehringhaus, granddaughter of a North Carolina governor, met her husband when he worked at the *Raleigh Times* in the early sixties. (The Raleigh paper, then owned by the Daniels family, often played mentor to the scions of other newspaper dynasties, Arthur Sulzberger, Jr., now publisher of the *New York Times,* being one such trainee.)

In pictures, Ayers and his father don't closely resemble each other. The Colonel looks more angular than his rotundish son. But Brandy, who likes to joke that his two major assets are nepotism and monopoly, insists he is very much made in his father's mold. The No. 1 rule for both: "My father told me not to get intoxicated with power. You don't throw your weight around. If you see someone abusing power, you're going after them with everything you've got. But don't do it yourself. Use power lightly and appropriately. Use it to oppose evil, not for revenge."

His wife smiles. "He's learned that lesson so well that not only does he not have grudges, he's sometimes disgustingly nice to people who say 'you should be wiped off the face of the earth.' I don't say he loves his enemies, but he finds them interesting." Some of the most vocal adversaries are invited to the paper's annual banquet honoring the best letters to the editor.

Asked for his strongest memory of his father, however, Ayers offers a personal recollection. The scene in which he sees his father most clearly has nothing to do with fame or principle or the paper. It's one that contrasts with the Southern male tendency to forgo overt affection. Ayers, then in the Navy, had driven part of the night and through the day to Anniston. He arrived in the middle of Christmas dinner. "Dad was so happy to see me, he embraced me." He didn't *overdo* the effusiveness. Welcome home, son, was all he said.

But Ayers and the Colonel were at odds in one major area: integration. "I came along in a different generation, and we differ. Racist demagogues set him off, but he couldn't take that last step. I don't think we disagreed on anything except that." And the sixties, of course, when Ayers was pulled home to help his ailing father, were very much about civil rights.

Ayers was in Washington, D.C., when the call came. To the young men and women caught up in Kennedy's Camelot, the view was one of eternal optimism, of possibilities for the common man, of both literal and figurative desires to shoot for the moon. And then Ayers was back in Anniston: "And it's on Old South time. And *your* views, thoughts, and conversations are radical." Sometimes the required readjustment was devastating. He wrote an editorial about blacks and the jury system. He thought it said what needed to be said. The town was horrified and infuriated. "And the dumbest thing," says his wife, is that "we were surprised."

Sometimes the two talked about moving away, about going somewhere where liberals were less exotic, where World War I memorials didn't separate the names of blacks and whites. But they stayed. They liked Anniston's natural beauty. They liked their house, their lives. They felt the pull of duty. It was, says Ayers, "the tug of nativity. This is *my* place. There is only one place that is *my* place."

They stayed—although Alabama, says Ayers, often has broken his heart. His memoirs will be somewhat of a social history about a state he terms "his first love and his greatest disappointment." The book's tentative title is "In Love with Defeat." The state can survive poverty and pellagra, he says, but "the thing that is unacceptable is the destruction of the human spirit." He talks about politicians' diet of scorn. He minces no words about Alabama's failures or what he sees as almost a psychosis induced by its undying opposition to the federal government. He's labeled the state "the Land of Oz— Oz-abama." Once he wrote that the New South had come to Alabama for a day in the form of five effective Southern governors there to talk about their accomplishments. A New South come *and gone* in a day, that is, because Alabama's own governor was out of town campaigning for the right to post the Ten Commandments in whatever public building citizens so desired.

Still, Ayers has hopes for his state. He calls its progressive Republican governor the best Democrat Alabama's ever elected. And he's proud that he's "honored my heritage, stuck up for the little guy, and taken a lively interest in what's happened to the world and translated that to Main Street." He's proud that he's been independent. He's proud, too, that even as all but about 250 of the nation's 1,456 dailies have been consumed by corporations, the *Star* has held on to family ownership. No lack of interest in the paper, sibling rivalry, or the lure of big bucks has tempted Ayers and his sister, Elise, as it has so many other owners, to sell.

Not that Elise or her husband, Phillip A. Sanguinetti, are political liberals—or even in danger of brushing the edge of liberalism. "My wife tells me I'm slightly to the right of Ivan the Terrible," says Sanguinetti, president of Consolidated Publishing, which runs the *Star* and its small affiliate papers. Elise, who worked briefly at the paper as a reporter, went to boarding school with Barbara Bush and is an avid Bushian. How have she and her husband avoided major clashes with their Democratic relative? "We just don't talk politics," says Sanguinetti.

He and Elise live in the white Dutch Colonial where she and her brother, who is eleven years younger, grew up. *Star* staffers are welcomed at pool parties there. Elise Sanguinetti is a novelist whose darkish views are well worth reading for what they reveal about the South of the sixties and seventies. And in her way, she seems as feisty as her brother. When a country club brochure amusedly claimed that Colonel Ayers had once punched a fellow member off its porch, for example, his daughter didn't rest until she had the offending item removed from future editions.

Ayers is in his seventies now, and no family member is waiting in line to take his place. Brandy and Josie's daughter, Margaret, who is in her thirties, works at the paper as a courier, and her new husband has just become a reporter there. Neither is a likely candidate to take the *Star* forward. The Sanguinettis have no children. But the Ayerses have a plan—a magnificent plan.

This is the legacy. In the 1930s, the Colonel decided Anniston needed a radio station. He started one. In the sixties, the family launched a TV station. But by the eighties, when the Federal Communication Commission decreed that no one media company could control its market, the Ayers family had to sell its broadcast outlets. The best thing to do, the family decided, was to find local owners, people who cared about Anniston's fate, people not strictly interested in the big bucks. The Ayerses sold the radio station at below-market value to two longtime employees. The TV station went to nearby Jacksonville State University, again at a bargain price. Shortly, both were resold to out-of-town interests. For the TV station, that meant a double-your-money, multimillion-dollar profit. The local connections had been severed.

No way that was going to happen to the *Star.* At first the idea was to give it to a university. But that, the family decided, would be the same as giving it to a political party. The *Star*'s independence would be compromised. Besides, the university might sell, just as Jacksonville State had done. The University of Alabama, of which Brandy is a graduate, was asked for ideas about how a partnership could work. "We were like two creatures circling each other," recalls Ayers. "We were clearly attracted but didn't know how to do the wild thing. We were getting pretty fed up with each other. The dean would say things like, 'What's in it for us?' That really irritated me. We were passing up $50 to $100 million."

Then in 2002, Chris Waddle, at the time the paper's executive editor, went to Miami for a meeting with university officials and the Knight Foundation, which was interested in bringing the two together. The meeting wasn't going well. "I was sitting there and looking out the window and saw what they call snow birds," he says. "It was surreal. It looked like they were coming to pick the pieces of failure." Then, suddenly, an idea. An idea that appealed to everyone. An idea that would become a reality. "The buzzards disappeared and everything started working."

Now Waddle is president of the Ayers Family Institute for Community Journalism and director of the Knight Fellows in Community Journalism. University of Alabama journalism professors and the paper's editors will work together at the *Star* and offer a free master's degree to twelve students. In its initial years, the university, the paper, and the Knight Foundation will put $2.75 million into the program. "We will be teaching life as it is lived," says Ayers.

The Ayers institute will sponsor other events, such as "The Angry World" panel and PBS-TV special, and whatever that world, and the world of journalism, seems to need.

Eventually, the stock of the paper will go into a not-for-profit foundation that will run the paper, turning most of what would have been the family's dividends over to the trust. The foundation's bylaws will prevent the sale of the paper. The *Star* will never become corporate. It will never be just one more link in a long corporate chain.

The people of Anniston will still have a local paper, a paper not driven by the interests of owners and stockholders thousands of miles away—an independent, not a homogenized, paper. A paper with an institute and a program that—remember this—focuses on *community* journalism. A product, be it on newsprint or the Internet or some as yet unimagined platform, that still "directs the current's flow toward 'will be.'"

"Our perpetual Christmas gift is meant for all—even the stinkers who paid us the compliment of passion, thinking we would hear and feel their criticism," Ayers wrote of the plan. He and his sister had an unspoken *understanding* with their father. The paper would not be abandoned. In 1985, on what would have been the Colonel's one hundredth birthday, Brandy wrote a front-page editorial spelling it out: Somehow, someway, the *Star*'s traditions would go on. He made his pledge: "That's a promise, Dad."

The promise will be kept.

Epilogue. The first six Knight Fellows came to the *Star* in fall 2006 to begin their teaching newspaper work for a master's degree. Bob Davis, who replaced Turner as editor in early 2006, says the fellows will assist on upcoming projects such as one on religion. The *Star* will explore in print, online, audio, and video how a person's culture affects his faith. It's a topic of special interest in a region where religion drives much of public life. University professors will simultaneously offer their take on covering religion and other project topics that emerge. The combination of real-life experience and academic depth enriches both.

Incineration of the chemical weapons continues. It's well on its way, but no end date is yet in sight. Activism against incineration has dwindled.

The Depot survives and thrives, not only missing the latest rounds of congressional closings but actually picking up several thousand jobs.

The *Star* continues to win state and national awards for work such as its series on asbestos litigation. "What's a Life Worth?" that one was called. The *Star* is still picking up community service, freedom of information, and Web site awards as well.

"My sense is we're going to continue the great standards set at this newspaper," said Davis. "But we're not satisfied with that great history. We work every single day to improve and to get better and to tell the story of this community."

Sources

To write this story, I talked in person with numerous residents of Anniston, staff members at the *Anniston Star,* and to H. Brandt Ayers, co-owner and publisher, the *Anniston Star;* Josephine Ayers, wife of H. Brandt Ayers; Scott Barksdale, executive director, Spirit of Anniston; Hoyt W. (Chip) Howell, mayor of Anniston; Elise Sanguinetti, sister of H. Brandt Ayers, and co-owner, the *Anniston Star;* Phillip A. Sanguinetti, president of Consolidated Publishing; Sherri J.

Sumners, president, Calhoun County Chamber of Commerce; Troy Turner, now the former executive editor, the *Anniston Star;* Chris Waddle, former editor, the *Anniston Star,* president of the Ayers Family Institute for Community Journalism, and director of the Knight Community Journalism Fellows, the *Anniston Star.*

My major phone interviews were with Pete Conroy, director, Environmental Policy and Information Center, Jacksonville State University; Jena Heath, editor, the *San Antonio Express News;* Clarence Jairrels, past branch president, NAACP, and last principal of Anniston's historic black high school; Edward Mullins, chair of journalism, College of Communication, University of Alabama; the Reverend Roosevelt Parker, past branch president, NAACP, and pastor, New Hope Baptist Church, Jacksonville, Alabama; Tom Spencer, reporter, the *Birmingham News;* Donald W. Stewart, attorney, Anniston; Cleo Thomas, Jr., attorney, Anniston.

In addition to the *Anniston Star* itself, other written sources include:

"Ayers Family Foundation to Support Journalism Education at UA." *Communicator* 26, no. 1 (2002).

Cobb, James C. "Community and Identity: Redefining Southern Culture." *Georgia Review* 50, no. 1 (1996): 9–25.

———. *Redefining Southern Culture: Mind and Identity in the Modern South.* Athens: University of Georgia Press, 1999.

Gates, Grace Hooten. *The Model City of the New South: Anniston, Alabama, 1872–1900.* Tuscaloosa: University of Alabama Press, 1978.

Gutwillig, Robert. "Six Days in Alabama." *Mademoiselle* (September 1963): 116–202.

Morgan, Tee. *Annie's Town: A Picture History of Anniston, Alabama, 1880–1940.* Anniston: Public Library of Anniston-Calhoun County, 1990.

Noble, Phil. *Beyond the Burning Bus: The Civil Rights Revolution in a Southern Town.* Montgomery: NewSouth Books, 2003.

Noland, Thomas. "Our Town: Our Stories." *Anniston Star,* October 14, 1979.

Risser, James V. "Endangered Species." *American Journalism Review* 20, no. 5 (June 1998): 18–36.

Stoker, Kevin Lamont. "Harry Mell Ayers: New South Community Journalism in the Age of Reform." Ph.D. diss., University of Alabama, 1998. Ann Arbor: UMI, 1998. 9831350.

———. "Liberal Journalism in the Deep South: Harry M. Ayers and the 'Bothersome' Race Question." *Journalism History* 27, no. 1 (2001): 22–33.

Turner, Thomas C. "Opinion, Please." *Mademoiselle* (December 1963): 38–42.

"What They Were Thinking." Photograph, *New York Times Magazine,* July 6, 2003.

Wesley G. Pippert

Watchdogs of Government Serve Citizens

The reporters who cover Washington are fulfilling one of the oldest and most important of journalistic responsibilities—watching government on behalf of the governed. In this chapter, you'll meet some watchdogs you've never heard of and learn how their work touches the lives of ordinary people across the country and around the world. The author, Wesley G. Pippert, is a veteran journalist with experience covering Washington, D.C. A professor at the Missouri School of Journalism, he directs the school's Washington Reporting Program.

When people think of Washington coverage, they often think of journalists like David Broder of the *Washington Post,* or Tom Friedman of the *New York Times,* or Helen Thomas, White House correspondent. Broder, the dean of American political writers, Thomas, a pioneering journalist who has covered every president since John F. Kennedy, and Friedman probably have more influence over U.S. foreign policy than most members of the State Department.

There are literally thousands of journalists in Washington. Between three thousand and thirty-two hundred are accredited by the Congressional Radio-TV Galleries. About two thousand are accredited by the Congressional Press Galleries. Of these, nearly three hundred also are members of the Regional Reporters Association, an organization set up in 1988 for journalists whose chief concern is what is happening in Washington that uniquely affects their local communities. About one thousand journalists are accredited by the Foreign Press Center, which is operated by the U.S. State Department to assist them.

These journalists face a common task: to let people know, whether in

America or abroad, what is happening in Washington that affects the people who will read or listen to what they have to say.

Here are some of their stories:

Protecting the Powerless

On May 19, 1953—a day that always haunted Isaac Nelson—a neighbor in Cedar City, Utah, called him outside to watch a huge, approaching fallout cloud from a government atomic bomb test upwind in Nevada.

His wife, Oleta, walked outside, too, wearing a short-sleeved dress and bobby socks. Neighbors chatted and marveled at the cloud from the test that later would be called "Dirty Harry" because of the massive, radioactive fallout dust it created.

Forty-five years later, Lee Davidson, then the Washington correspondent for the *Deseret Morning News* in Salt Lake City, wrote about the Nelsons' experience that long-ago day:

> They didn't worry about safety. After all, the government said the fallout was harmless. That night, Oleta suffered nausea and diarrhea. A headache struck that would pound for six months. . . . A few weeks later, Oleta "let out the most ungodly scream I've ever heard," Isaac said. "Half of her hair slipped off her scalp. . . . It never grew back.

> "Oleta died of brain cancer 12 years later."

In Nelson's mind, the government had killed his wife. He joined lawsuits against the government with other downwind cancer victims of the atomic tests. They believed there was a direct connection between those Nevada tests and the incidence of cancer.

The *Deseret News* carried stories about that connection and helped prompt Congress to pass 1990 legislation to formally apologize and compensate some of the victims of the testing. This made Nelson suffer again because the brain cancer that killed his wife was not among the types of cancer that the government said qualified for compensation.

A few years later, Davidson became the newspaper's correspondent in Washington. The *Deseret News,* with a circulation of about eighty thousand, was one of the smallest newspapers in the country to have a full-time correspondent in Washington.

Davidson decided to see how the law was working. Not very well, he learned.

The law had not been updated. More than half the people who sought compensation were denied. The government said they had the "wrong" kind of cancer or lived a few miles in the "wrong" direction to qualify. Some victims were unable to provide the kind of proof the government demanded.

Senator Orrin Hatch, R-Utah, used Davidson's stories to help update the law, including adding several types of cancer and making it easier for victims to prove their claims. Finally, in 2001, Nelson got his fifty-thousand-dollar compensation check—amounting to an apology he had sought for nearly half a century.

Davidson's work also disclosed secretive government chemical and biological weapons tests in Utah years earlier. He wrote:

> Throughout the Cold War, one corner of Earth was bombarded with nerve gas, germ warfare, nuclear fallout and other radioactive dust— spread to the winds by bombs, airplanes, artillery and even intentional nuclear reactor meltdowns. It was Utah.

Davidson kept digging and digging and came up with story after story, ranging from finding that the government conducted eight intentional nuclear reactor meltdowns in Utah to how it used Seventh Day Adventists (who were conscientious objectors to combat) as human guinea pigs in chemical and biological tests.

Davidson found documents showing that the United States had prepared through work in Utah to use chemical weapons in the World War II invasion of Japan (even though that would have violated international treaties), and dropped the idea only after the atomic bomb was developed.

Davidson first reported that secret U.S. chemical and biological testing at sea during the Vietnam War era had sickened many sailors. The Defense Department continued to deny this for years. Eventually the Pentagon acknowledged the at-sea tests and started helping the victims qualify for treatment.

Davidson kept on these stories—with little assistance or encouragement from the military. "The military is not helpful," he says. "They drag their feet."

But Davidson outwitted the wannabe keepers of government secrets. Among his colleagues in Washington, Davidson was known as "Mr. FOIA."

That is, he mastered use of the 1972 Freedom of Information Act, which allows citizens to have access to federal documents, except for those involving, for instance, national security or corporate copyright secrets.

Creatively, Davidson used FOIA from top to bottom—instead of filing one FOIA request to get a piece of information, he made requests at the Pentagon as well as at individual military bases.

Often, months later, Davidson would get the report he was seeking. The Pentagon's report, for instance, would be heavily excised. The same report he received from the military base also had portions that were blacked out—but not necessarily the same portions. So Davidson spliced the reports together and he was able to come up with a nearly complete report.

"Compensation never would have happened without these stories," Davidson said. Further, the military revamped its kinds of tests, and, as he put it, "the military is a lot more careful because of these stories."

Davidson's stories have netted him a long list of awards—plus a long list of more informed readers back home in Utah. The effect of his coverage on these people? "Over time it's created a culture change. Utahans are very patriotic and trusting. A lot of trust was squandered through these tests. There is less trust now. They don't want to be testing grounds any more. They're demanding more accountability."

Utahans praised his work. Chip Ward, cofounder of an organization called West Deseret HEAL (Healthy Environmental Alliance), said that many people at the time were hearing rumors about a lot of persons getting sick, a lot of cases of cancer, and were wondering whether there was any relation to the testing.

"Lee's stories were catalytic," Ward said. The stories helped raise consciousness in the community about the link between the environment and the illnesses. Ward said it's hard for a lay person to understand these highly scientific issues, but, he added, "Lee covered all this very well."

Revealing the Asbestos Cover-up

Greg Gordon, former Washington correspondent for the *Star Tribune* in Minneapolis and now national correspondent for McClatchy Newspapers, has written more than a hundred stories on the deadly effects of exposure to asbestos.

Asbestos was used for decades by carpenters, plumbers, pipe fitters, and other tradesmen to insulate pipes and boilers and as a fire retardant—meaning that uncounted persons get exposed. Lung diseases are caused by the tiny, microscopic fibers from asbestos, which float in the air and are inhaled, gradually scarring the lungs. What's particularly insidious is that symptoms typically don't appear for ten to forty years.

The statistics Gordon cites are stark: Asbestos could kill five hundred thousand American workers and result in three million injury claims—from an estimated twenty-seven million people exposed to it.

Gordon pored over hundreds of asbestos, insurance, and mining industry documents. He found that as early as 1929, an industry study of a manufacturing plant using asbestos in brake, clutch, and transmission linings disclosed one worker dead and several others too ill from asbestos-related diseases to work. According to a similar study, more than one in five Canadian asbestos miners and mill workers had asbestosis, a slowly progressive lung disease. Neither study was ever published.

Insurance companies tracked the disease but did little about it. After reconstructing the role of some of the nation's leading underwriters from mounds of court documents, Gordon wrote: "Some of the nation's largest insurance companies knew for decades that asbestos could kill but didn't warn workers or take other measures that might have averted the nation's worst workplace health disaster."

Frequently after Gordon wrote a story he was showered with e-mails and phone calls from afflicted persons. Over the years he has interviewed two hundred of them, often by telephone. Few reporters in Washington are as skillful as Gordon in working the phones to get information.

Gordon told of a sign outside the Western Mineral Products Company in northeast Minneapolis that said "FREE CRUSHED ROCK." It was near an inviting waste pile of processed vermiculite ore. Folks in the neighborhood and throughout the Twin Cities, Gordon wrote, loaded the ore to spread on their driveways, gardens, and barbecue pits. They had no inkling that the vermiculite was contaminated with deadly tremolite asbestos.

One man, Mike Janowiec, remembers how he and his buddy, Harris Jorgenson, and other kids played "king of the mountain" in the pile of light and squishy waste. Jorgenson died at age forty-four, his family believes from the effects of the tiny fibers embedded in his lungs from the times he played on the rock pile.

Most asbestos exposure takes place in manufacturing or industrial plants, but the Minneapolis rock pile led to community exposure.

The tainted ore came from Libby, Montana, where vermiculite ore was mined for generations. Dust from the ore had sickened and killed hundreds of miners and residents in Libby in the worst community asbestos exposure in the nation. Contaminated ore was shipped throughout the country, including to several plants in the Twin Cities.

Gordon found that Minneapolis probably was second only to Libby in terms of community contamination. Physicians, lawyers, and family members told him that asbestos exposure had contributed to the deaths of at least thirty persons who worked at or lived near Minneapolis factories using vermiculite.

His stories led the U.S. Environmental Protection Agency to declare a former W. R. Grace and Company plant in northeast Minneapolis and many nearby homes a toxic waste cleanup site. The Minnesota Department of Health cleaned out the waste pile and obtained federal funding for a survey of 6,400 past and present residents of the neighborhood. The study found that 655 persons had played on that waste pile. The Minnesota agency credited Gordon's stories for prompting the action.

"His articles made a positive contribution to public health by bringing the Minneapolis Western Minerals/W. R. Grace site to our attention and alerting citizens," said Rita Messing, a supervisor in the Minnesota Division of Environmental Health. "When the press 'sets the public agenda' in this way, they pave the way and garner support for our work in the community, specifically our investigation into community exposures to vermiculite waste from the facility and finding contaminated property. This attention also motivates both local, state, and federal government players to participate in the process of finding solutions."

Dennis McGrath, then national editor at the *Star Tribune,* praised Gordon's persistence in covering the asbestos story. "Greg drove home the connection between something happening in Montana to what was happening in Minneapolis."

"Greg got lots of reaction from people all over the country," McGrath said. "That's satisfying."

Connecting with People Back Home

Not all Washington stories deal with life-and-death issues.

When Sylvia Smith became the Washington correspondent for the *Fort Wayne Journal Gazette,* she was determined to make the nation's capital more accessible to the people back in Indiana. Smith had been a senior editor at the *Journal Gazette* for several years before she was assigned to open its one-person Washington bureau in 1989. She knew her readers. So she soon wrote a story on how a typical family of four in Fort Wayne could spend a three- or four-day vacation in Washington for less than five hundred dollars.

Smith scoped out inexpensive motels. She went to the parking lot at the Pentagon City subway stop and made note of the shuttle buses from nearby motels. Then she called the motels to see which were the cheapest. She suggested that the family eat the motel's continental breakfast, take a sack lunch with them, and stop at a fast-food restaurant in the evening. She pointed out that many things in Washington are free—such as the Capitol, the Smithsonian, and a nighttime military band concert. She calculated the amount of gasoline and tolls it would take for the twelve-hundred-mile round trip between Fort Wayne and Washington. Total cost? "$499 and some change," she said.

Davidson, Gordon, and Smith are among the several hundred "regional reporters" in Washington who report for individual newspapers on developments in the nation's capital of particular interest to their home communities. In fact, they probably spend most of their time covering their state's congressional delegation or other typical Washington stories. Many of these regional reporters have not lost their conviction that the Washington stories that are important are those that touch people's lives or strike a responsive cord like Smith's travelogue. And, not all of the stories coming out of Washington affect people in such life-and-death ways as what Davidson and Gordon wrote about.

Many of Smith's stories, for instance, are more policy-oriented. Here, too, she delivers for the folks back home. These days members of Congress, sometimes in another attempt to circumvent the Washington press corps, often have conference calls with reporters back in the state. As Smith points out, these reporters often have one or two burning questions. What she can ask, that the locals probably would not, is the more probing third question or fourth question.

Smith knew that the business community in northern Indiana was interested in the Hoosier Heartland Corridor project, which would stretch east-west on U.S. 24 across that part of the state. One day Smith was covering a Transportation Appropriations subcommittee hearing. Representative Jill Long was there to ask for funding for the corridor. It crossed part of Long's district, but the corridor mostly reached across the district of then-freshman Representative Steve Buyer. Buyer was not present for the hearing. Later, Smith bumped into Buyer and asked why he didn't attend the hearing that was dealing with a project important to him. He told her he didn't know about it. Later, Smith wrote a column about it, pointing out that Buyer, whether out of lack of information or indifference, was absent. Business people in Buyer's district let him know they were not happy about his absence, and from then on, to be sure, he was present when the project was discussed.

The editors of the *Journal Gazette* say that they—and Indiana readers—have responded enthusiastically to Smith's reporting.

"Before Ms. Smith went to Washington, the coverage of members of our congressional delegation pretty much consisted of rewriting their press releases, covering the campaigns, and interviewing them when they visited the hometown," says editor Craig Klugman. "Now, we can put their work in accurate perspective—knowing what the congressman's, congresswoman's, or senator's real contribution is."

Says managing editor Sherry Skufca: "The value of Sylvia Smith's coverage to our readers is in direct proportion to her hard work as a veteran journalist in developing this beat and the network of sources she needs to localize—yep, localize—what is happening in Washington, D.C. . . .

"In short, she thinks like our readers think in northeast Indiana and northwest Ohio. She asks the questions they would ask. She puts it in a perspective that is meaningful at home. And she writes for our readers. Many of the names in her source file began as readers who called, wrote, or e-mailed her directly."

Covering for Television

Brooks Jackson, whose thirty-six-year career in Washington stretched from the Associated Press to the *Wall Street Journal* to CNN, thinks like a voter.

Many people see politics, particularly political campaigns, as simply bombastic jargon and believe that politicians' actions frequently don't match their rhetoric. Jackson long has looked behind and beyond their words and deeds to see the role of money. In 1992, during the presidential primaries, Jackson was one of the first television correspondents to analyze campaign ads for accuracy. His spots became known as Adwatch.

Jackson sorted out those ads making factual claims that could be checked, as contrasted to those with sweeping, ambiguous statements such as "it's time for a change." He found few outright false ads, but he did find far more that were misleading or incomplete. During a presidential campaign, Jackson said, he screened about 20 percent of the candidates' ads, and only half a dozen times did he actually label an ad as false. "I didn't strain to call it false," he said. "I didn't find people lying very often—but twisting the facts, much more often."

Jackson recalls he received a few letters. "Some were mad when I went after their favorite politician and didn't care much about the facts. Others just seemed to appreciate that somebody was trying to sort through all the bullshit and tell it to them—the voters—straight."

He got plenty of reaction from other sources. Tom Hannon, CNN political director, said that if one of Jackson's spots was critical, almost immediately the politician's ad maker contacted CNN in protest. Soon, however, the ad makers began to provide documentation, often within the ad itself. The Radio and Television News Directors Foundation (RTNDF) began a series of workshops on covering campaign finance at several places throughout the country. Jackson's efforts were spilling over on news directors from coast to coast.

"A lot of stations elsewhere in the country have now made this a part of their routine," says Deborah Potter, executive director of RTNDF and herself a former network correspondent.

Even back home in Indiana, Jackson always had had an interest in the visual—which he appropriated in his challenge at CNN—how to talk about money and corruption on television, the medium, ironically, that contributed to the excesses. He knew that reporting on money and politics always is done more easily in print than on TV. After all, to show a list of the top fifty donors or recipients is possible in print but impossible on television. A person can scan a newspaper's list of one hundred names to see where a particular congressman is found—but it's not possible on television to show any more than the top three or the top five. It's very difficult to report adequately on TV about such things as corporate greed or cooking the books or balance sheets.

Jackson's interest in following the dollar—"I'm less of a storyteller than an accountant," he says, "I like to look at the figures and see if they add up"—burst into print a generation earlier during the Watergate break-in and cover-up. Probably the worst political scandal in American history, Watergate started innocuously during the 1972 presidential campaign at the Democratic party headquarters in the Watergate complex in Washington's Foggy Bottom neighborhood. White House Press Secretary Ron Ziegler initially called it "a third-rate burglary." But as the months wore on, thanks to the diligent work of *Washington Post* reporters Bob Woodward and Carl Bernstein, the nation learned that if President Richard Nixon did not know about the break-in before it happened, he was deeply implicated in trying to use the CIA and FBI in a futile attempt at covering up high-level involvement. Eventually, Nixon resigned, the various Watergate trials ended, and the nation moved on to other political stories.

Jackson went beyond the obvious. If Watergate was a story of how the intense desire to propagate one's political power had led to corruption and crime, it may be even more true that Watergate portrayed, even climaxed, the change in America from a rural, small-town country with mom-and-pop stores and small-town high schools to an economy of huge, powerful corporations that use money and influence to get their way. In short, Watergate capped the economic and social revolution that had been taking place in this country. And in retrospect, this may be fundamentally what Watergate was about.

Jackson covered this historic aspect of Watergate. He began digging and writing about how the break-in was financed. Others had reported how cash, in hundred-dollar and even thousand-dollar bills, from Nixon's flush Committee to Re-elect the President was used to pay the "plumbers," the infelicitous sobriquet attached to the break-in team that had been set up at the paranoid White House to stop "leaks" to journalists. Jackson followed the money.

Soon a broader pattern of financial abuse was revealed. The Associated Milk Producers Inc. was a cooperative dairy so large it processed much of all milk products between Minnesota and Mexico; AMPI promised a $2 million contribution to Nixon's campaign, while the president was granting them higher federal price support for raw milk. Jackson's coverage won him the Raymond Clapper Award for Washington reporting.

The "milk fund" stories revealed that corruption tainted the Congress as well as the White House, and Democrats as well as Republicans. The Nixon campaign illegally accepted corporate funds from the dairy farmer lobby, but so did the campaigns of Democratic presidential candidates Hubert Humphrey and Wilbur Mills.

The story of campaign finance is still with us more than a generation later. Television and computers, meanwhile, have changed politics. Computers made possible and simplified the use of targeted ads and targeted mailing lists. Coupled with the cost of television ads, politicians must raise huge amounts of money.

"We can't deny we have an Arab perspective in our coverage," he says. "But there is an American perspective, for instance, at CNN. We expect American television to focus on American victims. When we have Palestinians killed, we focus on them and their suffering. They matter to our people the same way Jessica Lynch (the American soldier who was liberated as a prisoner of war in Iraq) matters to the American people."

Persuading people of its commitment to balance has not been easy for Al Jazeera, Al-Mirazi says. "Because we cover both sides of the story, we've been vilified by all parties."

The ruler of Qatar, Sheikh Hamad b. Khalifa Al-Thani, founded Al Jazeera in 1996 as a network modeled after BBC, Al-Mirazi says, and most of the original staff came from the BBC Arabic service. Its signal, although aimed primarily at forty-five million to fifty million viewers in the Arab world, reaches throughout the world. North Americans can watch an English-language version of Al Jazeera on some cable services or satellite services or through its Web site. Al-Mirazi joined Al Jazeera in 2000, he says, only after getting assurances that he would stay with the new network "as long as it was a balanced and objective outlet."

"The irony is that at VOA it was my assignment to give an Arabic perspective to the story; at Al Jazeera it is my assignment to give an American perspective."

Al Jazeera has covered what Al-Mirazi refers to as "civil rights issues," such as the passage of the Patriot Act after 9/11 and the criticism it has aroused on grounds it violates basic liberties. The purpose of this coverage is clear: "because of what Arabs and Muslims in America have been subjected to, immigration, visas," Al-Mirazi says.

As far as encountering resistance in its coverage in the United States, Al-Mirazi says, "we've been treated fairly." He adds, "In some cases, we run into someone who's not nice to us. And sometimes they (the U.S. government) try to use the offer of interviews as leverage to affect coverage."

Yet, Al-Mirazi feels there is a "double standard" practiced in American journalism. He holds up two examples—the running of pictures of bodies of people killed in the Iraqi war and tapes of Osama bin Laden.

Al-Mirazi said the Pentagon did exactly what it criticized Al Jazeera for doing. He said the Pentagon—and the American media—ran at length the hatred-filled tapes of bin Laden talking to his followers with English subtitles in attempting to connect him with 9/11. A short summary would have sufficed, in Al-Mirazi's opinion. As for the photos, the Pentagon criticized Al Jazeera for running them. Yet, the U.S. government later made photos of the bodies of the two sons of Saddam Hussein available to the media specifically for showing to the Iraqi people.

Since Al Jazeera's emergence on the scene, we have seen a proliferation of Arabic news and general channels. A remarkable two channels per month are emerging on Arab networks. "This plurality of stations is a clear example of the freedom of expression that is emerging on the airwaves—at least in the rather unrestricted satellite market," says Richard Eisendorf, an expert on Middle East media.

"What may rile Americans about Al Jazeera's and other Arab channels' coverage of Iraq is the partisanship of their editorial tone," Eisendorf says. "But it reflects the general sentiments in the Arab world, suspicious of American intentions in the Middle East, critical of America driving the war in Iraq, rejecting America's role in occupying an Arab country."

Al-Mirazi expresses these thoughts. "What was the difference between the graphic pictures that had been released by the Iraqi government to Al Jazeera and the graphic pictures released by the U.S. government to Al Jazeera and other networks?" Al-Mirazi asks. "This double standard undermines the whole message coming from the U.S."

In a nation like America, where freedom of expression constitutes a huge part of what we consider a democracy, a healthy mix of opinions, even critical ones, is vital.

It will be up to journalists in Washington to make sure that the flow of relevant information and argument continues to reach the citizens of the world. They must follow the examples of these reporters:

• To keep burrowing into old, traditional beats while, on the other hand, to keep asking, "what's new?" as Howell did.

• To tell the story in ways that let average people know how they are affected by a new federal regulation or act, while at the same time communicating enough of the technical details of the decision or legislation, as Gordon and Davidson do.

• To avoid seeing coverage of government as merely coverage of Congress, state legislatures, county commissions, city councils, or even school boards. For often these groups have become little more than debating fora, while faceless, anonymous uncovered bureaucrats in the departments and agencies are making decisions every day that affect people.

• To show the courage of reporting even in the midst of occasional hostility or resistance, as Sean Naylor and Hafez Al-Mirazi do.

The good news, of course, is that the people can be confident they are getting—or will get—the story out of Washington. During the Senate Watergate hearings at the height of the cover-up, John W. Dean III, the former White House counsel turned source, testified quoting an old English proverb, "the truth will out." He, of course, proved correct.

Sources

Material about the journalists in this chapter was based on personal interviews with each of them between 2003 and 2005 along with a study of their work over an extended period of time. The author also drew on his own decades of experience as a Washington reporter and director of the University of Missouri's Washington program.

Some of the material was taken from the author's article in the University of Nebraska's *Journalism Alumni Review* for the summer of 2005.

Journalism Builds New Democracies

Americans often take our First Amendment freedoms—our freedom of religion, press, speech, assembly, and petition—for granted. We often take for granted as well the journalism freedom allows. In countries suffering the birth pangs of democracy, journalists who regularly risk their own freedom to provide the independent reporting required by people who would govern themselves are just now earning those freedoms. Meet some of these unsung heroes. Author Byron Scott is professor emeritus and former director of international programs at the Missouri School of Journalism. He has lectured and consulted with journalists and journalism educators in forty-seven countries, including those represented in this chapter.

Once they made black-and-white movies about journalists like these. Past generations huddled around their radios, listening through the static to their fictionalized exploits.

• A crusading investigative reporter, risking her life to expose corruption.

• A small-town newspaper editor, publishing the truth on an economic shoestring and winning readers' hearts along the way.

• A broadcaster fighting racial prejudice to become a respected editor on a nationwide network.

• Another journalist, trying to find the objective truth from both sides in a war where the "first casualty" is always the truth.

Today's entertainment media tend to portray contemporary journalists differently, often as venal, cynical, self-centered—and American. Some of the world's most admirable journalists are not Americans, although they are very real. In fact, the four just described are not only real but are Kosovan,

Albanian, South African, and Palestinian. They are among the new generation of journalists, emerging in nations under transition throughout the world and dedicated to improving their nations from behind a camera, microphone, or computer.

This chapter looks at the lives of those four journalists working in nations on the edge of our geographic consciousness, doing solid journalistic work, sometimes at the risk of their own lives. They are part of a generation who know the values of good journalism and who, out of the limelight, are doing things that might be rejected by contemporary movie and TV scriptwriters as not real. Here are the stories of that investigative reporter, Fatmire from Kosovo; that crusading small-town editor, Lushi from Albania; that battling broadcaster, Jeffrey from South Africa; and the courageous Walid, a Palestinian who works in Gaza and the West Bank.

Their stories remind us that, in the United States and other developed Western nations, we take press freedom for granted. In 2006, the International Federation of Journalists said there was a record 155 killings and unexplained deaths of journalists. While the constitutions of virtually every one of the world's more than two hundred nations "guarantee" press freedom, the enforcement of this basic right is often lax. In many nations, those same guarantees also link critical journalistic performance to criminal penalties. In others, journalists are the special targets of criminal and civil elements who don't want truth told. A camera on the shoulder may be "mistaken" for a rocket launcher. An assassination attempt on an investigative reporter is dismissed as "a drunken incident" by local police.

That's what happened to Fatmire Terdvice in November 2004. Fatmire, who looks even younger than her barely thirty years, was eight months pregnant when the drive-by shooting took place. Winding over the pitted roads of Kosovo near Pristina, the journalist was a passenger in a car driven by her brother. Another car, which had been following them for miles, suddenly pulled alongside. Shots rang out. Terdvice was wounded in the right arm. Her arm remains stiff, but she is able to hold her son, Leka—named after the son of King Zog, Albania's twentieth-century monarch—who was born several days later. The would-be assassins, dismissed by police as joy-riding drunkards, were never found.

A journalist for only seven years at the time of the attack, she is already a well known and, in certain circles, cursed investigative reporter in the Balkans. She is small, even a bit short by regional standards, and might be mistaken for a teenager when she smiles, but her usual expression is grim concentration. Her daily newspaper *Koha Ditore* (Daily Times) has about thirty thousand readers in both Kosovo and abroad. In a time when politics, war, and ethnic strife have killed or changed the careers of most of her generation, she is considered a "senior journalist." The average age of her colleagues is just twenty-one.

She would like to remain an investigative reporter for at least another ten to fifteen years and then perhaps become an editor or teacher. She has a boyfriend but feels it is unfair for them to marry, in part because of the danger inherent in the stories she reports. "Maybe I'm an idealist, but you have to think you may not have safety. A policeman or a soldier is the same as a journalist many times." In Kosovo that may be an understatement.

Years after the end of the civil conflict that briefly moved it to the world's front pages, Kosovo remains a tense, corrupt, and often dangerous place. Most of the burned and bombed buildings have been rebuilt, but Pristina, the capital, has the aura of decay and despair. For years the presence of more than forty-five hundred international policemen/peacekeepers, the forces known as UNMIK and KFOR, reinforced the sense of an occupied war zone. Most of the two million Kosovans, 90 percent ethnic Albanian Muslims and the rest Orthodox Catholic Serbs, believe that the United Nations and international NGOs, not themselves, run Kosovo, which remains against its will as part of Serbia (formerly Yugoslavia). There is a resigned sense of inevitability and even permanence. The adult unemployment rate hovers around 60 percent. Many feed their families by smuggling anything from cars to cigarettes, drugs to oil and, of course, women. "Kosovo is a paradise for investigative journalists," Fatmire says with a wry smile.

Only among friends will Fatmire talk about her reporting techniques. To strangers she may enigmatically say only: "When you do this work, people come to you." Too many Balkan journalists are merely collectors of gossip, blindly publishing whatever they hear, regardless of source credibility. Fatmire likes to see things for herself.

For example, there was her investigation of the oil smugglers' pipeline in Peja. The international embargo of Serbia, like all such blockades, was extremely leaky. Mountains, corruption, and generations of Balkan tradition kept vital supplies flowing to the Milosevich regime. One particularly blatant method was the Peja pipeline, which literally ran across the Albanian/Serb frontier at a major customs checkpoint. Each night, tanker trucks pulled up on one side and pumped their loads into the partially camouflaged pipe for the short trip down a ravine and up into similar trucks on the other, Serbian side of the border. Of course, civilians were kept away by police and customs officials. But Fatmire had to see and photograph "what everybody knew."

She persuaded an older friend, a policeman, to take her into the ravine on several occasions where she took pictures and counted trucks. One night they were caught. "He told everyone I was his mistress and, of course, they believed and congratulated him." What better spot for a lover's tryst? "No, I did not bribe the policeman to take me there. I never pay my sources. They might make up information only to sell it. . . . He agreed with me that this (smuggling) was harmful to our future."

At least once, Fatmire had to ask for police protection although her editor, like many recognizable leaders in the region, has his own bodyguards. She was reporting on the abduction, rape, and subsequent death of an eighteen-year-old schoolgirl. Witnesses of the abduction, as well as neighbors of the house where she was briefly kept, identified the abductor as the son of a prominent family. After her release, the girl, shamed by her experience, poisoned herself but left a note identifying the same man. Dismissing it publicly as a lover's tragedy, local police never completed an investigation. They even refused to pick up the official report of the girl's autopsy that detailed evidence of rape. After regional officials issued an arrest warrant for the man, these same police refused to serve it. "Kosovo was without law at this time . . . It was totally a vacuum," Fatmire notes, adding that the current situation is only marginally better.

Against her editor's counsel, Fatmire decided that she could not publish her story without confronting the accused man. He needed the chance to tell his side of the story, she insisted.

Reluctantly, the editor sent his own bodyguard with her. The accused refused to see her, but a brother promised: "I will kill you if you publish this story." The story was published and she walked the streets of Pristina with a policeman for a while afterward. "I had to stop that. No one would talk to me," she recalls. No prosecutions resulted from the case, however. But in a land where vendettas were born, memories are long.

Fatmire has done dozens of these stories in recent years. Most have had no official response. A few, exposing corruption among UNMIK and KFOR troops and officers, including Americans, Germans, and even a Bangladeshi, have resulted in the embarrassed recall of the men to their home countries. But, in general, she reports in an environment where crime and corruption are considered part of "the current Kosovo reality." Why does she continue? Part of the answer comes from her family, who "always taught me that nothing worth working for is ever easy . . . including justice."

Among the most difficult things was something Westerners take for granted: going to college. In 1993, just turned eighteen, she won admission to the school of journalism at the University of Tirana in neighboring

Albania. At that time the Serbian government had closed the university for ethnic Albanians in Pristina, so her entrance exam had to be taken through an underground "parallel process."

But the governing Serbs refused to allow her, an ethnic Albanian, to leave the country. She twice tried sneaking across the border and was caught. Then she and her father took an old smuggler's route through the mountains into Macedonia and then to Albania on foot. When he returned weeks later, authorities accused Fatmire's father, a power company engineer, of smuggling and took away his passport for three years. Fatmire, who returned to Kosovo only after graduation, was granted her first passport in 2002. "I broke up the fear a long time ago, on that walk through the mountains," she explains.

The Crusading Editor

Albania, where Fatmire Terdvice earned her university education, is no bastion of independent journalism, a free press, or free speech. The history of Albania as a nation is short and troubled. After declaring its independence from the Austro-Hungarian Empire in 1912, Albania became a nation following World War I, only to become a bloody monarchy for less than a dozen years. What followed after World War II was the xenophobic, trust-nobody dictatorship of Enver Hoxha. Albania was the last Balkan nation to reject communism in the early 1990s after decades under the despotic Hoxha and his followers.

Our crusading editor, Engjellush "Lushi" Serjani, lives and works in Hoxha's hometown, the ancient and beautiful southern Albanian city of Gjirokaster (sometimes spelled Gjirokastra). A castle, built by rulers of the Ottoman Empire, overlooks the town of perhaps thirty thousand people. In the early nineteenth century, English poet and adventurer Lord Byron (George Gordon) was the honored guest of Ali Pasha and waxed rhapsodically about the rugged beauty of the town, little valley, and mountains he saw from that place. But for most of the last half of the twentieth century, the castle was a prison where Hoxha sent political prisoners. The townspeople say that Hoxha liked to sit in the garden of his Gjirokaster home on summer evenings, listening to the screams of his tortured opponents and enemies. But Hoxha and his brand of communism are dead and gone, and Lushi doesn't print unconfirmed stories.

Bespectacled, roly-poly, with not much hair and a big, seemingly omnipresent smile, Lushi is arguably the most respected journalist in southern Albania. As editor of the weekly *Dita Jug* he also until recently headed the only newspaper in the region. He is the perennial president of the professional journalists organization that represents the diverse audiences of ethnic Greeks, Macedonians, and Albanians that populate the region.

Albania is more than 80 percent mountainous. Most of the winding roads have not been rebuilt since the Second World War. All of the nation's daily newspapers are published in Tirana, the capital, and usually arrive in places like Gjirokaster a day or three after publication. Television and radio, whether local or national, are sporadically received and "news emissions" are frequently interrupted by electrical power failures, especially in the winter. But word of mouth travels rapidly in all seasons. The people trust most what they hear from their neighbors. Lushi is a trusted neighbor.

Copies of the weekly paper are eagerly anticipated at the kiosks of Gjirokaster's main boulevard and most of the twelve hundred copies sell out quickly. But Lushi always keeps an extra stack in the back of his battered Ford Bronco. Miss this week's issue? Bought a loaf of bread instead? Never mind, here's a free one.

Lushi seems always on the move. His vehicle is his real office as he honks his horn and waves like an American country politician, stopping frequently to joke, laugh, and listen. It's not unusual to see the Bronco blocking traffic as Lushi communicates with his readers. The town traffic policeman sticks his head in the truck's cab, asking the editor to move on. Instead, Lushi grabs the dangling whistle and blows it. Everyone, including the policeman, pedestrians, and most of all Lushi, get a good laugh.

Lushi gets the news wherever he goes. People tell him things, knowing he doesn't publish gossip. Instead, he gives the information to his staff to check out. Western newsrooms have never seen a group of reporters like this one. About a dozen at any one time, they are part Baker Street Irregulars and part Robin Hood's merry band. Most are self-taught journalists. Lushi is their combination editor, mentor, and father figure. Happy, friendly, and willing to work all hours of any day, they get paid only when the paper can afford to give them something. Reporters range from a retired professor in his sixties to several students who began writing for *Dita* in high school and are now at the local university. Lushi's second-in-command is Genna, a serious woman in her mid twenties who is also news editor at the local state-run radio station.

The paper works out of a pair of tiny rooms, about six-by-nine feet each, in the Communist-era "press building," now largely unoccupied, unheated, and vandalized by locals who stole windows, doors, and furniture when the government fell in 1997. Western media managers would see no sense in how the paper works. There are no set working hours for anyone. The staff shares a couple of cell phones and Lushi always seems to know where they are at critical times. Everyone does everything, from getting pizza to taking photographs with a taped-together digital camera.

Friday is deadline day. Staffers happily jostle each other to write their stories on two computers in the tiny office. There is always a bottle of the potent Albanian homemade brandy, raki, around to cut the chill. Klidi Proko, the art director, a university student who sleeps on a mattress in the next room most of the time because his home village is too far away, lays out the paper on a third PC. Everyone hopes the power doesn't go off.

In the controlled Communist system, the decision to generate both heat and light nationwide exclusively by hydroelectric power seemed to work. But now demand has outpaced a decaying grid. Despite the promises of succeeding governments, electrical power in Albania became a sometime thing. The farther from the capital and the colder the weather, the more unreliable the light and heat. Six to eight hours on winding roads from Tirana and separated from the warm waters of the Adriatic by a low mountain range, Gjirokaster can get very cold indeed.

If all goes well, Klidi finishes laying out the new issue in the early evening. But routinely that doesn't happen. When the lights go out in Gjirokastra, Lushi has three options: wait it out in the dark and cold office, lit only by a candle; fire up the staff flashlight and lead the staff down the darkened stairs and out to some café that can afford a generator for an impromptu staff meeting and party; or, if only a few more moments are required, bribe the electric company.

If that third option seems appropriate, Lushi grabs a bottle of raki, steps across the road to his friends at the local electric complex, and—voilá—the lights go back on for a few precious moments. Before 2003, when an international media organization gave them a printing press, the editors had another prepublication ritual. Then, Nyazi Sako, the only other staffer who has a car—he is also the southern Albania correspondent for a national TV channel—took the printouts and disk containing the precious pages to be printed. It was more than fifty miles by road to the nearest printer. As Nyazi roared off, Lushi and the staff customarily shared a celebratory drink. Lushi, who speaks minimal English, toasted them all with his favorite phrase: "Good. Very good."

Somehow, *Dita Jug* is always back on the streets again for the Saturday shoppers and feeds the café conversations for another week.

Without Lushi and his weekly paper the Turkish coffee and raki-drinking conversations so important in Gjirokastrans' daily lives might be pretty tepid. Most weeks there is a new scandal, problem, or project to report. As a former Tirana newsman who still reports to the big city's papers on local news, Lushi is tied securely into the information pipeline. He also is known for his carefully researched "little exposés." One example involved a local contractor and politician who received a rare but lucrative government contract for a new apartment building. Shortly after its completion, the structure showed evidence of shoddy workmanship: leaks, cracks, and crumbling plaster included. Lushi also heard that the rooms were smaller than anticipated.

In common with virtually all transitional nations, Albania lacks public record laws that in the West allow journalists to look at plans, contracts, and the like. Lushi ("I have friends") was able to get copies of the key documents that confirmed both the materials used and the structure's size itself were slightly less than the contractor's claimed expenses. Abounding denials from the contractor and officials who had approved the structure did no good. The public had seen photos of the official documents in *Dita Jug*. At least for a while, there were no new contracts for Lushi's target.

On another occasion, officials loudly insisted that the only road bridge into the older part of the city was as sound as when it had been built nearly two centuries before. When the paper published photos showing extensive cracks on its underside—taken with the taped-together digital camera—the road was closed to trucks pending repairs.

Lushi began his career as a Tirana journalist, but he and his wife moved to Gjirokaster in the early 1990s to raise their family. In the old days, still so very recent, the Albanian media was owned and controlled by the state. Today, virtually every daily paper in Tirana represents a political faction. Independent journalism is best done in a place like Gjirokaster, Lushi insists. He will never be rich, but he is content.

Sometimes they think about moving back to Tirana. That thought was very strong after a cold evening in mid-December 2005 when two unknown assailants beat Lushi unconscious. Lushi recovered but now is more aware that his readers include enemies as well as friends. Still, he remains upbeat.

While his wife, Violeta, a librarian at the local university, bustles in and out of the kitchen of their apartment, Lushi shares a breakfast of fresh bread, cheese, wild cherry jam, and coffee with a friend. His young daughter colors in a preschool exercise and his son cruises in and out of the room on roller skates. "Is good?" asks Lushi. Then he answers his own question: "Good. Very good."

Emerging from Apartheid

The award-winning British journalist and analyst Misha Glenny has observed: "If the fire of prejudice could be doused with a potion of tolerance, the Balkans would be the most wonderful region in the world." Journalists like Lushi and Fatmire are doing much to achieve that goal with even-handed journalism that is blind to race, religion, or ethnicity. They would probably like Jeffrey Twala.

The place and the nation where he is a broadcast journalist, Cape Town, South Africa, are half a world away from Pristina and Gjirokaster. But many of the same problems and challenges exist for journalists and the societies they serve.

Jeff, currently Cape Town news editor for South Africa's national broadcasting network, has been a journalist for more than twenty-five years. For most of that time he was also a second-class citizen in his own nation. Until 1994, South Africa and its institutions, including the state-operated South African Broadcasting Corporation (SABC), operated under apartheid. He is black.

Sitting in his office overlooking a public Atlantic beach that now allows all races, Jeff still looks like a somewhat heavier version of the all-star rugby player who attracted SABC recruiters over a quarter of a century ago. Atop a stocky body, his thick and muscular shoulders support a thick neck worthy of an American football lineman. His large head and prominent forehead complete the profile that earned him his rugby nickname, "The Black Rhino."

Some of his contemporary SABC coworkers still call him by that nickname, Jeff acknowledges, but not to his face. "They may be forgetting. I've had to have a thick skin for a long time. Like the rhino." After leaving his village, Jeff paid his own way through school as a well-regarded rugby player and then as a regional broadcaster of the games themselves. SABC, seeking to attract black audiences, took notice and hired him as the first of his race on the network staff. He was an employee but not a peer of his fellow journalists.

The post-apartheid Truth and Reconciliation Commission, chaired by

Anglican Bishop Desmond Tutu, published an extensive description of how black journalists at SABC and elsewhere were treated by their apartheid-era editors and coworkers. They could not eat in the company cafeteria and, if meeting a white colleague in the hallway, were required to flatten themselves against the wall. The penalty for black journalists who argued the judgment of white editors, or who did not step aside in corridors, was to be fined, suspended, and even to be beaten. "They never beat me," Jeff says with a slight smile. "But I was never able to eat where the others ate. They even built a separate place for me to use the bathroom, out in the parking lot."

In the post-apartheid South Africa the new government policy is to build a "rainbow society" marked by equality. The daily reality of "The New South Africa" is finding ways to get along in government-run institutions like SABC, usually with black leadership. More than half a million white South Africans, primarily Afrikaans, have not been able to accept that situation and have emigrated, primarily to England, Holland, and North America. Jeff was appointed to his current job over senior, white journalists who once were his bosses. He is now in charge of more than thirty black, white, and "colored" (mixed-race) radio and TV journalists. His daily tasks are as much diplomatic as journalistic, and everyone, including Jeff, knows it.

Jeff speaks in short, uncomplicated, direct sentences. Only part of that is his radio background. He wants everyone to understand his opinions and instructions. "You can question Jeff's news judgment," one of his white subordinates notes, "and he'll listen. But he always knows what he wants and so do you. He's always the editor. You'd better not forget that."

The bureau's twice-daily assignment meetings reflect that communication pattern. In most respects they resemble those taking place in American newsrooms but with the additional subtext of nation-building and recent role reversals. Jeff and the on-duty news editor have just been participating in the nationwide "line call" of all SABC bureaus. They talk about what's going on in South Africa today and how their bureau will be part of those stories. Reporters present their own ideas. Then Jeff and other editors give assignments. The national junior rugby team is being announced. It's important, notes Jeff, that the story "answers questions about the fairness of the selection process." He doesn't have to explain what he means by fairness.

Every SABC journalist must be at least bilingual. The network broadcasts major shows in English, Afrikaans, and Hausa as well as regional shows in Swahili and major tribal dialects. South Africa has nineteen official languages. Each day, SABC broadcasts in thirteen of them. Each journalist is accustomed to interviewing, writing, and editing their stories in more than one language and for both radio and TV. Often, the biggest challenge is neither linguistic nor media-related, however. It's cultural sensitivity.

The longtime head of radio news for SABC, Pippa Green, summarized the journalistic challenge in a 2004 article in the U.S.-published *Nieman Reports.* With an audience that is at least eight times larger than the largest newspaper's, SABC's daily challenge is intimately linked with the future stability of the nation. Green points out that the protected status of SABC as a public broadcaster, funded overwhelmingly by traditional commercial fees and ads, was established a full year before the Mandela government even attempted free elections. "Ten years into democracy, many journalists are struggling to redefine their relationship to government. It is not the government of old, easily defined. . . . Neither—though many in the cast of characters are the same—are they comrades of old who were on the same side of the barricades as journalists who covered their fight against apartheid."

Jeff likes to try to shock his visitors with questions like: "How would you like it if I moved into your neighborhood, then decided to let my ancestors know where I am by slaughtering a bullock in the yard?" He means to say that today's South Africans are mixing but will need much effort, time, and understanding before the process becomes at all comfortable. The examples are there in every news cycle.

On a bright April morning the students at Zola Secondary School have returned from a holiday break to find flooded classrooms. Someone has turned on a water spigot in the second floor of the school in the huge Cape Town township of Khayelitsha (New Hope) and left it on for days. There will be no school today for more than a thousand pupils, grades seven to twelve.

At the morning news meeting, Jeff assigns a "colored" reporter and white photographer to cover the story. They drive to the school and find hundreds of neatly uniformed students milling around in the shadeless courtyard. Inside, the principal, head in hands, is refusing to talk to angry parents and journalists alike. He is awaiting word from his supervisor, as well as the arrival of the councilor for Khayelitsha, an official in the African National Congress.

The reporter and photographer assess the situation, pick up the cell phone, and call Jeff. "There's no story here . . . probably vandalism . . . happens all the time." The reporter spends the next few moments holding the phone inches away from his ear, but listening carefully. This is a story, Jeff tells them. The black people in the townships need to know that SABC cares what's happening to them. If this happened in a white school . . . ? The journalists go back inside and interview the principal, whose supervisor insisted he should remain silent, as well as the parents and the ANC representative. It's a local story, but one that wouldn't have been done in earlier years.

"Small stories are often remembered," Jeff explains succinctly. "Not every story is important throughout the nation, but it may mean more to some elsewhere in the nation that we did cover them." Jeff is in the middle of a cross-cultural experiment that involves an entire nation. The results are still in doubt. But he and his colleagues are convinced that how they do journalism will be an important factor.

Treading a Fine Line

Walid Batrawi is the son of a journalist. Israelis and Palestinians in high places have called him a son of something else. A correspondent for the BBC Arabic Service, based in Ramallah, he is a rare professional who, in the process of reporting daily on the shootings, bombings, and tensions of his native region, strives for balance, frankness, and honesty in his reports. In 2003 he was recognized by the world's largest reporters' organization, the International Federation of Journalists and the European Commission, with the prestigious Natoli Prize for Reporting Human Rights, Democracy and Development in the Arab world.

Born in Jerusalem in 1969, Walid grew up in a journalist's household. His father, Mohammed, was editor-in-chief of the Palestinian daily *Al-Fajr* (The Dawn). In common with the children of many journalists worldwide, Walid reached adulthood wanting to do anything else. Like many bright Palestinians of his age, Walid won a scholarship to study in Moscow. His field was to be civil engineering. But the turbulence of the Arab-Israel tensions got in the way.

Returning to the West Bank, Walid became a guide-cum-interpreter-cum-diplomat working with Western journalists covering the conflict. He became what is known as a "fixer." In areas of conflict, particularly war zones, a reliable "fixer" is an indispensable guide, translator, and aide for international journalists who often rush to the story without the native language or good backgrounds on the culture, history, and politics of the region. Walid was a superb fixer who soon found himself doing journalism.

When the first Gulf War, repelling the Iraqi invasion of Kuwait, broke out, he was a cameraman for the First Channel of France (TF1). Later he moved to the Jerusalem Media and Communication Center, which became a trusted independent voice on the media and the continuing conflict between Palestinians and Jews. Over the years, working out of Ramallah on the West Bank, Walid became a well-known TV producer for the Australian Broadcasting Corporation, among others.

He and his wife, Benaz Soniry, a journalist specializing in women's rights, produced several documentary films as well as the first Palestinian news program aired live from East Jerusalem.

Walid's voice became familiar, often with gunfire in the background, on Pacifica Radio and NPR. His reports, rather than taking a militantly pro-Palestinian approach, tended to be balanced but descriptive of what really happened. Walid's friends cherish a photo of him, standing in the middle of a street, clad in flak jacket and steel helmet, grinning broadly at the word "PRESS" printed across his chest. In the background an Israeli tank approaches.

When asked about his reporting in the West Bank, Gaza, and elsewhere, his response is succinct: "My work is fine, difficult and dangerous, as usual." Among the problems is the high-octane mixture of nationalism and frustration that suffuses everything in the region. Palestinian journalists are expected to be anti-Israeli and pro-independence in their reporting. Even though a Palestinian, Walid refuses to comply. As a result, neither side seems quite sure how to handle him.

Little has changed for reporting in the region since the death of Yasser Arafat and subsequent elections. Journalists generally lack professional skills, which is compounded by a lack of information, he notes. Under breaking news conditions, special preference is given to the government-backed media such as the Palestinian Broadcasting Corporation. Often there are only unofficial sources, all saying different things. "The Israelis are perhaps a little easier to deal with," Walid notes, "because there is currently less tension."

On-the-street reporting takes up most of Walid's time, but he also teaches a course in online journalism at Bir Zeit University, which sits on a hillside just outside Ramallah and is periodically closed by Israeli troops. The professional education of future Palestinian journalists is the special responsibility of people like himself, he believes. "I learned journalism from my father and then from reporters who came here to report our troubles," he notes. "I have something to pass on." In the summer of 2006 Walid announced that he was becoming a correspondent for the Qatar-based Al Jazeera Network but would remain in his hometown of Ramallah.

Doing Journalism under Difficult Conditions

By definition, good journalists are interested in people. But often journalists forget how interesting the individuals they work alongside can be. Jeff, Fatmire, Lushi, and Walid are engaging professionals who, because of day-to-day difficulties, are somehow more interesting than journalists in developed countries. When Woodward and Bernstein reported the Watergate scandal, they likely never worried about how their stories would affect the future of the United States. The Watergate story brought down the Nixon presidency, but it did not bring down the country. Journalists in transitional nations do think about the ramifications of their work. Too many become propagandists seeking power; others go for quick-profit gossip mongering. But a recognizable group is doing good journalism under difficult conditions that sometimes endanger their lives as well as their livelihood. That they do as well as they do without the resources—professional, economic, and legal—of their Western colleagues is inspirational. They remind us of how important journalism can be to a civil, stable society.

This chapter could have looked over the shoulders of journalists from many other such nations who have the courage to practice journalism:

• The young Bulgarian TV journalist who shocks her nation and its prime minister when, after he has issued a lengthy, florid statement on government-sponsored TV, she chases after him to take the unprecedented action of asking a question. As Bulgarians watch, he wheels, stares into the camera, and gives a direct, honest answer. Then he turns and flees—into the men's bathroom.

• The editors in Northern Ireland who, secretly meeting with Republic of Ireland counterparts, agree on more temperate language for describing incidents within "The Troubles." Terrorists will now be called "para-military groups," etc.

• The Russian editor who, knowing he will lose the town's advertising that feeds his budget and his family, writes about drunks in the streets and drugs sold in doorways, asking: "What are we, as citizens, going to do about this?" Several months later he is stabbed while unlocking the door to his apartment. He dies in his wife's arms.

• An editor in Ulaanbaatar, Mongolia, shivering at his desk and writing an editorial by hand. Over his head in a battered frame is Thomas Jefferson's famous quote: "The basis of our government being the opinion of the people, the very first object should be to keep that right; and were it left to me to decide whether we should have a government without newspapers, or newspapers without a government, I should not hesitate a moment to prefer the latter."

But those are other stories.

Sources

The journalists profiled in this chapter were interviewed over a period of months from 2002 to 2004. Follow-up inquiries were conducted over the Internet. The *Nieman Reports* article quoted appeared in the Fall 2004 issue.

The author met, interviewed, and observed these unknown heroes in their homes and workplaces.

Investigative Reporting Saves Lives

Of all the important roles played by journalism in a free society, investigative re-
porting is both the most demanding and the most crucial. Investigative reporters dig
below the surface of events and issues to expose failures and reveal wrongdoing. Their
work often leads to reform and always to greater public understanding. Although
journalists in the United States do not usually face the kinds of threats that we read
about in the previous chapter, they do confront economic and political pressures. And
they rely on the legal protection won by generations of predecessors. Author Brant
Houston is executive director of Investigative Reporters and Editors Inc. and a pro-
fessor at the Missouri School of Journalism.

The problem was obvious and it was lethal. In case after case, courts were
overturning the wrongful convictions of Illinois prison inmates on death
row. Yet, no one seemed willing to look at the systemic causes of those er-
roneous charges, prosecutions, and convictions. And so, with officials failing to take action, the *Chicago Tribune* decided to examine every death sentence in the state.

Steve Mills, one of the three reporters involved in the investigation,
wrote after the *Tribune* published a package of illuminating and deeply trou-
bling stories:

> We sought to test the premise that the system worked. . . . We
> pulled at the threads that ran through the cases that appeared em-
> blematic of the system's troubles: bad lawyers, jailhouse snitches,
> flawed forensic science. The work resulted in a series of stories that
> changed how Illinois' criminal justice system was viewed, and changed

how reporters cover the courts—bringing a new skepticism to how the justice system operates.

In fact, the governor, citing the *Tribune's* stories, declared a moratorium on executions. The Illinois Supreme Court changed key court rules for handling capital punishment cases, and the state legislature also has made reforms.

The work didn't end there. Since the initial publications of stories in 1999, the *Tribune* has written stories on every part of the criminal justice system, including examinations of false confessions, the execution of innocent inmates, life after exoneration, and, most recently, forensic science. The *Tribune's* work also inspired other journalists to do similar investigations with the same high standards of thoroughness and attention to detail. Most important, because of that work, innocent men walked out of jail to start new lives, some for the better, some for the worse, but none of them was put to death for crimes they did not commit.

The *Chicago Tribune* series is one of thousands of stories that show investigative journalists play a critical role on behalf of the public by keeping governments and businesses accountable for their actions.

In doing so, journalists often question authority, challenge the powerful, examine the fairness of the status quo, and ask whether there are better ways of living in society. Sometimes, as shown by the *Tribune,* a news organization can actually save lives.

Acting as society's watchdogs, investigative journalists speak out when the public is in danger because of lax rules or toxic products. They also speak out when the weak are being abused by the strong. And they often serve as the court of last resort for people who have tried every other way to attain a remedy for a social ill or injustice.

The leading group in the field, Investigative Reporters and Editors, defines investigative journalism as: "The reporting, through one's own initiative and work product, of matters of importance to readers, viewers or listeners. In many cases, the subjects of reporting wish the matters under scrutiny to remain undisclosed."

What is not spoken of in the definition is the close relationship and collaboration that often develops between journalists and the public on these stories. If no official or business will listen, your best chance at getting your concerns addressed is to find an investigative reporter. And if you are an investigative reporter, you are dependent on the help and conscience of those who care deeply about justice and fairness and share an outrage about wrongdoing.

Because of this, investigative journalism distinguishes itself from routine journalism through this special relationship to the public and through its attention to accuracy, fairness, and completeness. The techniques and standards of investigative journalism can be used in all news stories, but frequently reporters don't have the time or training to meet those standards. In fact, in an effort to constantly improve the quality of its stories, investigative journalism has embraced over the past decade the techniques of other professions, including those of police, lawyers, private investigators, forensic accountants, and social scientists.

The use of data analysis—known as computer-assisted reporting—has been particularly beneficial. With social science methods, investigative journalists have brought more context and depth to stories and actually succeeded in doing stories they could not have done before without skills in analyzing data. (See chapter 8.)

Because of their willingness to take the time to thoroughly understand a topic, investigative journalists can dissect a larger and more complex issue and help bring about change when needed. Among the many issues probed by other investigative journalists in the recent past have been:

- Widespread shortcomings in the criminal justice system
- Flaws in the child-care system
- Abuse and exploitation of the elderly
- Lax medical procedures
- Dangerous practices in the pharmaceutical industry and failure of regulators to prevent those practices
- Failures in preparing for natural disasters.

In each of these areas, journalists found governments and businesses unable to police themselves. Thus, the public relied on the journalists to expose the problems and put pressure on officials and corporations to rein in abusive practices. The journalists sometimes spent as many as ten months on stories. Their employers spent tens of thousands of dollars on salaries, purchasing and analyzing data, travel, and copying documents. In one case, ABC's *20/20* investigative team spent $12,500 to ensure fifty rape kits were processed so that rapists could be tracked down.

The Criminal Justice System

The *Chicago Tribune* was far from alone in its reporting on wrongful prosecutions and convictions in the past decade.

KHOU-TV in Houston has an investigative team that has consistently aired important stories ranging from shoddy health-care practices to the revelation of serious and fatal defects in car tires, which led to major reforms in the auto industry.

The KHOU-TV investigative team, headed by veteran reporter David Raziq, produced some of its greatest work when it found that the Houston Police Department crime lab had been making serious mistakes in its testing for years and that the flawed testing led to innocent people going to prison and guilty people going free.

In recounting how they did the story, Raziq and reporter Anna Werner said the flaws had gone unnoticed because prosecutors and defense attorneys had implicitly trusted the scientists. But one defense lawyer did notice the crime lab was having problems with one of its forensic tests and tipped off reporters at KHOU.

In their preliminary investigation, the team eventually met with an independent forensic scientist who said she had alerted authorities to the lab's problems, but no one listened. Team members then dug through criminal cases and interviewed lawyers and others in the legal system. They quickly saw that the lab work was not being double-checked or "peer reviewed." With the help of experts, the team established that there had been "repeated gross incompetence."

In less than a year, Raziq and Werner said, the probe "resulted in the shutting down of the DNA lab, more than a thousand past criminal cases getting new DNA testing of crime scene evidence," and the removal and forced retirement of several police officials.

The *Seattle Post-Intelligencer* conducted a similar investigation of the Washington State Crime Lab in 2004. Again, the results were shocking. The newspaper uncovered forensic scientists producing false results that enabled prosecutors to send many wrongly accused persons to jail. Furthermore, reporter Ruth Teichroeb found that even when the scientists' methods were challenged and their work discredited, those falsely accused stayed in jail. Once again, it took an investigative reporter's work to expose the injustices and lead to cases being overturned and scientists removed from their posts.

Nationally, reporters with *20/20* revealed another shortcoming in the testing for criminal cases. In their investigation, they reported that it was not a problem of bad testing, but of no testing. They discovered hundreds of thousands of rape evidence kits sitting unprocessed in police storage rooms across the country. ABC journalists said police told them the kits were unanalyzed simply because there is no money to process them.

To test the police claim, ABC paid half the cost to process DNA from fifty unsolved rape cases selected and handled by the Baltimore police. There were four immediate matches on four cold cases. In one case, a rapist was arrested and pleaded guilty. Two cases involved one rapist, who pleaded guilty. In the fourth case the testing cleared an innocent man who had been wrongly jailed for a rape he had not committed.

After the story, the Baltimore Police Department received $700,000 from a private foundation and the city government to process its entire rape kit backlog. For the citizens around the country, the story resulted in new funding from government and private foundations to process rape kits. Former New York City Commissioner Howard Safir created the National Rape Evidence Project, a private foundation created to steer private funds to law enforcement agencies to process rape kits.

Child Care

Another area in which the investigative journalists have worked on behalf of the public in recent years is in child care. In the first years of this century, reporters focused on officials and agencies responsible for taking care of children. Instead of just reporting on single instances of abuse or neglect, investigative journalists have again looked at how a system breaks down.

In Florida, reporters at the *Sun-Sentinel* in Ft. Lauderdale responded with an intense effort when state officials at the child welfare agency said they could not locate more than five hundred children under its care. Some of the children had been missing for ten years or more. The reporters wanted to know whether the state simply wasn't trying to find the children.

As a test, reporters looked for twenty-four of the children. They found two children within three hours. Within a few days, they located one boy the state said had been missing for eight years. Within a few weeks, they had found nine of the twenty-four children. They found the children by examining public records and interviewing relatives. Within a short time, the head of the Department of Children and Families—the child welfare agency—resigned, and the state began instituting reforms to prevent the lax practices of its employees.

A governor's task force set up to locate the missing children found hundreds more of them. The task force also produced thirty-four recommendations to make it easier to locate missing children by limiting the secrecy of the agency files and making the agency share information on missing children with other states.

In a major investigation with large-scale ramifications in the nation's capital, the *Washington Post* unveiled "critical errors" in the city's social system. It documented the actions of officials that led to the death of forty children who were supposedly under the protection of social workers, police officers, judges, and other city employees.

In its investigation, the *Post* acquired confidential files that showed how widespread the neglect by city officials was. Reporters said one in five of the so-called protected children who died "lost their lives after government workers failed to take key preventive action or placed children in unsafe homes or institutions." Furthermore, the newspaper found that confidentiality laws drafted to protect children were actually used to protect government officials from scrutiny.

The series began after the *Post* had reported extensively on the beating death in 2000 of a twenty-three-month-old child who had been sent by a judge back to a neglectful mother. The reporters on that story learned that the child was one of many who had died while in the care of the District of Columbia.

Through interviews and the documents searches, the *Post* detailed the fatal shortcomings of the system and spurred significant reforms.

Among the results:

• The city established its first licensing regulations for foster and group homes.

• Officials resigned or turned over control of cases.

• Funding for child care increased by millions of dollars.

• Congress passed legislation requiring federal judges to create a family court division to better handle the cases of neglected and abused children.

In Colorado, the *Denver Post* used documents and databases, along with multiple interviews, to track precisely the defects in that state's child protection system. Reporter David Olinger revealed that 41 percent of child abuse fatalities were "preceded by warning calls to protection agencies." He also found the state fatality review team often failed to investigate and report the prior warnings. And like other reporters, he saw that officials again used confidentiality laws, not to protect the children, but to cover up their mistakes. The outcome of Olinger's work was the creation of a child abuse commission that pursued improvements and better fatality investigations throughout the system.

The Elderly

While one group of investigative journalists revealed and helped to relieve the dangers children encountered, other reporters have been exposing the abuse and exploitation of the elderly. Journalists revealed shoddy care in group homes, the hiring of violent criminals as caregivers, and con men and guardians who were taking advantage of the trusting elderly clients and customers.

In a series of stories, *Newsday* in Long Island, New York, exposed the neglect of mentally ill elderly patients at assisted living centers in their region. Reporters said they discovered a frightening litany of problems. Some ill patients were allowed to wander miles away from the centers. Others failed to get their medications. Some were attacked by center staff members or other patients.

The story began when readers complained to the newspaper about the quality of assisted-living care. The reporters and editors said they quickly realized they were in unfamiliar territory because so little had been done on the treatment and care of elderly people with Alzheimer's disease or other forms of dementia. Although there were a limited number of documents, and family members were initially reluctant to talk, the newspaper built one database with details on more than one hundred facilities and another database on health department violations. They matched the two databases to track where problems were and to guide them to key interviews. The journalists concluded that the assisted-living industry was overlooked in "a patchwork of regulation" and that regulation was so poor that some centers had not even been licensed.

The legislature acted on the findings. Four months after the series ran, state legislators passed a comprehensive assisted-living bill that required the licensing and inspection of assisted-living facilities and the certification of those who dealt with elderly dementia.

News organizations in Detroit, St. Louis, and other cities recently have pursued stories that seek to protect the elderly. The *Dallas Morning News* produced one of the most notable public service stories.

In "State of Neglect" reporters detailed the failure of the Adult Protective Services, the state agency created to care for Texas's senior citizens who have mental or physical disabilities. The newspaper reported that many of those vulnerable people were living in "rat-infested, human-waste-strewn filth" and were prey for sexual predators and financial exploitation.

As part of its investigation, the newspaper examined more than thirteen hundred probate court cases in which the agency requested guardians for the elderly or emergency action. The newspaper interviewed probate court judges, police, attorneys, advocacy groups, relatives, and social workers and acknowledged the investigation could not have been done without the help of judges and court investigators.

After the stories appeared, the push for reform in guardianships and improvement in elderly abuse investigations increased quickly. Probate judges created one task force to push for funding a county program in the Dallas area and another to create a better safety system for the elderly. The state legislature later approved a bill that increased the agency's funding to hire more caseworkers. In addition, the Dallas County commissioners agreed to spend $95,000 to provide guardianship services for the first time for vulnerable adults.

Unsafe Medical Care

More reporters have decided to probe unsafe medical care as the public has become more wary of how the care is delivered and the kind of care that is provided.

At the *Hartford Courant* in Connecticut and the *Daily News* in New York, reporters have chronicled how bad doctors have continued to practice despite disciplinary action and lawsuits.

Investigative journalist James B. Stewart in his book *Blind Eye* showed the systematic failure of the disciplinary action by tracking the path of one killer doctor who transferred from hospital to hospital across the United States despite officials' knowledge that the doctor was a danger. It took a judge tipping off Stewart to bring full attention to the doctor.

One of the most powerful investigations by a newspaper was the *Chicago Tribune*'s two series by Michael Berens on hospitals. One demonstrated how the lack of training for nurses and nurses' aides and poor nursing practices led to at least two thousand deaths throughout the United States. The other showed how infections contracted at hospitals resulted in deaths and diseases for thousands more.

In the second series, the *Tribune* reported that seventy-five thousand of the infections in one year were preventable but that hospitals were not taking adequate precautions.

Since then, hospitals have launched major campaigns to reduce the number of infections, and nurses pushed for reforms, successfully getting a ground-breaking minimum-staffing law in California. In addition, the Joint Commission on Accreditation of Healthcare Organizations began a national crackdown on the use of potentially deadly infusion pumps exposed in the series.

Pharmaceuticals

Over the past decade, investigative journalists have not only improved their coverage of care for the young and old but also have upgraded their ability to deal with the complex and peril-fraught world of legal drugs. They have looked into the questionable practices of the industry and the doctors and pharmacists who prescribe and distribute the drugs.

While in general the government keeps the public informed of prescription drugs that are found to have serious or fatal side effects, it does not routinely report on the loopholes in its own regulations. At the Knight-Ridder bureau in Washington, D.C., reporters Alison Young and Chris Adams investigated cases where patients had been prescribed drugs by their doctors for conditions other than that for which the drug was developed.

"An asthma drug for pre-term labor? A powerful anti-psychotic as a sleep aid?" Young and Adams wrote when recounting their work. "Such uses may strike consumers as odd, but for the medical community, they are an everyday thing."

The reporters found the number of "off-label" drug prescriptions increasing and dangerous. The drugs were called "off-label" because the Food and Drug Administration–approved instructions on the label do not include those uses. The reporters found that the FDA doesn't regulate the practice of medicine, and doctors are free to prescribe an approved drug for any reason. They also found that most of the "off-label" prescribing is encouraged by marketing and "sloppy medicine." For example, they found that 70 percent of the retail sales of an epilepsy drug were for conditions other than epilepsy.

To look at the wider problem, however, they reviewed twelve years of prescription data from the Centers for Disease Control and purchased prescribing and sales data for sixty drugs. They also examined the FDA's database of adverse reactions and saw numerous reactions caused by "off-label" prescriptions. One immediate result of the series was that the FDA took the rare action of requiring that all prescriptions for the heart drug amiodarone carry stronger patient warnings including detailed information on its approved uses because the series exposed its widespread off-label use. At the federal veterans affairs department, officials used the stories to help review off-label use in the department's national hospital system.

Meanwhile, the *Washington Post* also examined the drug system and produced a series showing how "a corrupt network of criminals and profiteers has infiltrated the nation's drug supply chain, buying, stealing and counterfeiting many of the lifesaving medications that wind up in America's medicine chests."

Longtime investigative reporters Gilbert Gaul and Mary Pat Flaherty tracked an international multibillion-dollar illicit enterprise whose practices have led to death and injury to patients who had no idea that they were getting counterfeit drugs. One woman profiled in the series (and who later died) had received a diluted, repackaged cancer drug.

The series started when the reporters came across felons who had bought millions of dollars in prescription drugs. By going through court records, business documents, and other filings, they were able to begin to put together the pieces of the clandestine operations. Then they began identifying Internet sites where drugs were marketed and sold and matching that information to state pharmacy records and incorporation papers. More research revealed that some doctors, who had disciplinary actions filed against them by medical boards, were writing prescriptions for Internet sites.

The series immediately prompted efforts at reforms from regulators, Congress, and trade groups. Within days, drugstore.com, the largest legitimate online pharmacy, announced a public campaign to alert consumers to the dangers of rogue online pharmacies. Some of the large search engines such as Google and Yahoo said they would revamp their advertising links to dangerous, addictive prescription medicines. Google specifically said it would stop accepting ads from unlicensed pharmacies cited in the *Post.* Some of the major interstate shippers also said they would review their policies for handling the shipment of painkillers from Internet pharmacies.

In Florida, Fred Schulte, a reporter at the *Sun-Sentinel,* discovered other problems with doctors and pharmacies. Schulte documented cases of unsuspecting patients dying of overdoses of legal drugs because doctors and pharmacists were willing to distribute large amounts of narcotics. Using autopsy records and police records, Schulte recounted how the reporters traced the drugs that ended in fatalities and the doctors who prescribed them.

"State officials lack a system to do this [investigate deaths and doctors], even though they admit that a pattern of deaths may warrant disciplinary action against a doctor," Schulte wrote about the investigation.

Schulte used Medicaid billing data with drug overdose files to show that many of the doctors receiving high Medicaid reimbursements for drug prescriptions of narcotics were the same doctors associated with a high number of patient deaths.

Spurred by the reporting of Schulte, the state placed restrictions on the licenses of five doctors and filed manslaughter charges against another doctor. The Florida attorney general credited part of the investigation with forcing a settlement in a lawsuit against drug manufacturers. The settlement of the state's investigation into the companies' marketing tactics required the payment of $2 million to build a databank that allows officials to track narcotic prescriptions in Florida.

On a national level, *Los Angeles Times* reporter David Willman probed the development and approval of drugs. Willman, who has done numerous stories about the drug industry, looked at the relation between drug companies and doctors working at federal agencies. Willman outlined how payments from drug companies to scientists at the National Institutes of Health cause conflicts of interest that can adversely affect health care and policy recommendations.

In his investigation, Willman unveiled how the National Institutes of Health allowed its scientists to take side jobs as consultants for drug companies. Willman showed how this conflict of interest affects the scientist's work and how it can be detrimental to the health of citizens in the United States. He found that the agency not only allowed this conflict of interest but also permitted top-paid employees to keep their consulting confidential. He continued working on the story and later reported that even under the partial reforms announced by the institutes' director, some NIH scientists would still be able to take compensation such as stock options and consulting fees.

As a result of his reporting, NIH employees were finally formally banned from taking consulting fees and stock options from biomedical companies. In addition, hundreds of additional NIH employees are now required to file annual financial-disclosure reports that are open to public inspection.

Disasters: Predicting and Preventing

Investigative journalists have become more sophisticated at dissecting disasters, whether man-made or natural or a combination of the two, and providing potential solutions. In recent years, the journalists have gone far beyond just reporting the facts of transportation and infrastructure disasters in their attempt to protect the public from other deaths and injuries from the repeated problem.

As far back as 1981, the *Kansas City Star*'s reporters were able to reveal within twenty-four hours the cause of a hotel's walkways collapse that killed 114 people and injured more than 200. Through a key source and scrutiny of building inspection documents with an expert, the newspaper identified the fatal building design flaw months before federal officials issued their report. The newspaper also continued the investigation to show how a fast-track schedule and lax building inspectors contributed to the collapse. The efforts spurred better regulation and closer attention to building design.

In the early-1990s, investigative journalists at the *Miami Herald* compared building damage reports after Hurricane Andrew with wind speeds to pinpoint where shoddy construction had been allowed in the region. The exposé resulted in improved building codes throughout Florida and elsewhere.

In the mid-1990s, journalists' attention turned to airline crashes and mishaps. With the help of numerous databases on aircraft and their mechanical problems, reporters, moving much quicker than government and business, showed patterns of design weaknesses or explained the probable causes of crashes.

Bryan Acohido of the *Seattle Times* focused on rudder problems of 737s as the cause of one major crash in 1994 and other close calls through interviews and reviews of aircraft databases. Acohido reported that the rudder system on the 737s sometimes can malfunction and make the airplane dangerously difficult to control. In 1996 he did a comprehensive report on the overall problem.

Also in 1996, Beth Marchak of the *Cleveland Plain Dealer* disclosed how the Federal Aviation Administration ignored mounting safety and maintenance problems at several carriers including ValuJet airlines. The FAA waited until six weeks after the crash of ValuJet Flight 592 killed 110 people to ask the airline to ground itself, even though at least four inspections of the airline showed repeated safety problems were neither fully investigated or corrected.

Long before September 11, 2001, when terrorists flew airliners into the World Trade Center and the Pentagon, journalists wrote about airport security lapses. In the late 1980s, broadcast investigators reported on lax security throughout the airport industry. Among the many stories before

9/11, WCPO in Cincinnati reported in 1996 that its investigation had "un-covered major holes in airport security, behind the scenes where the public can't see." It revealed that a Delta subcontractor employing hundreds of people in high-security jobs at the Cincinnati/Northern Kentucky Inter-national Airport did not always do the required background checks. The undercover investigation revealed "that almost anyone could be hired, and once hired, it would be possible to sabotage a plane."

Over the past decade, investigative journalists have tried to warn the public about the threats that hurricanes present to growing coastal areas.

Some of the most startling stories appeared in the *Times-Picayune* in New Orleans. In 2002, three years before Hurricane Katrina slammed into the city and surrounding communities, the newspaper ran a perceptive and frightening series of stories on what would happen to the city if a strong hurricane struck. The overview read:

"It's only a matter of time before South Louisiana takes a direct hit from a major hurricane. Billions have been spent to protect us, but we grow more vulnerable every day."

A summary of the second part of the series said:

"A major hurricane could decimate the region, but flooding from even a moderate storm could kill thousands. It's just a matter of time."

These stories were followed by other similar examinations in such pub-lications as *Scientific American, National Geographic,* and the *New York Times.* Yet government officials did not act, and when Hurricane Katrina hit the region in 2005, it killed more than one thousand people, punched holes through the city's levee system, and flooded the streets of New Orleans. The watchdog had barked, but government officials turned a deaf ear.

After the hurricane, the *Times-Picayune* and other news organizations then began to ask questions about the lax response by government agencies and the qualifications of those who ran them. The *Washington Post,* for example, reported that five of the eight top officials at the Federal Emergency Man-agement Agency had "virtually no experience."

Reporters at the *South Florida Sun-Sentinel* continued to work on stories on FEMA they had begun years earlier and found "the handling of aid to victims of Hurricane Katrina is only the latest in a series of missteps and fraud that has plagued this tax-funded government agency." The newspa-per looked at twenty recent disasters and said "mismanagement and mis-allocation abound."

To obtain their findings, the reporters analyzed one million claims for the twenty disasters and created maps showing the location and amounts paid.

The Future

As these stories show, investigative journalism plays an integral role in alerting a free and democratic society to problems. It also suggests possible solutions for the better in its work. Sometimes, officials listen and make changes. Sometimes they do not. If informed citizens don't follow up by demanding reforms, government often refuses to act.

In the coming years, with the increasing use of the Internet to share information and to probe deeper into how systems work, the investigative journalist and members of the public will work more closely together. With one e-mail to a newsgroup, a journalist can solicit help for an investigation. With one e-mail a member of the public can reach an investigative journalist with not only a tip but also information to back up the tip.

Together, investigative journalists and the public will continue to throw a spotlight on injustices and abuses, but at a much quicker rate, with a wider distribution of their findings, and a much better chance at attaining a better society.

Sources

The content of this chapter comes from information from several archives in the IRE Resource Center. They include investigative news articles, contest entry forms on how those stories were accomplished, tip sheets on news coverage from IRE conferences, and articles on investigative journalism from the *IRE Journal*. Other material was drawn from archives from a conference on watchdog journalism that was held at the Poynter Institute for Media Studies in 2005 and from e-mail interviews with investigative reporters and editors including George Papajohn of the *Chicago Tribune*, Maud Beelman of the *Dallas Morning News*, and Deborah Nelson and David Willman of the *Los Angeles Times*.

Online
IRE Resource Center including news stories and tip sheets
    http://www.ire.org/resourcecenter/
IRE Journal Archives
    http://notes.ire.org/resourcecenter/irejournal/index.html
Poynter Institute for Media Studies including archives from watchdog journalism conference
    http://poynter.org/content/content_view.asp?id=83381

Computer-Assisted Journalism
Creates New Knowledge

In the last few years, journalists have found another tool to monitor government. That tool is computer-assisted reporting. By using computer databases of public records, journalists are able to monitor the performance of government agencies and to check claims against statistics not previously available publicly. David Herzog, who as director of the National Institute for Computer-Assisted Reporting has trained many journalists across the country, and Brant Houston, executive director of Investigative Reporters and Editors, explain how this technique serves you, the reader.

For years, journalists had listened to stories about African American motorists pulled over by the police and arrested for "driving while black." The journalists could report on the drivers' anecdotes of unfair treatment, but they lacked solid information to show that the arrests were part of a systemic problem and not aberrations from otherwise solid police work. There was no way for the public to know for sure: Did the police disproportionately target the black drivers?

Now, thanks to a relatively new reporting technique called computer-assisted reporting (CAR), journalists have answered the question.

In 2004 NBC's *Dateline* aired "A Pattern of Suspicion," a report that found police across the country citing black drivers for driving without a license or failing to wear a seat belt at a rate that exceeded the one for whites by more than three times. *Dateline* discovered the racial chasm only after analyzing more than four million traffic stops and tickets in more than a dozen U.S. cities from coast to coast. The news program built its own database and then discovered the story hidden inside it.

"These guys have done a terrific service to tell the story in a thoughtful, complete way," said David Harris, the Balk Professor of Law and Values at the University of Toledo College of Law. Harris has written about racial profiling, worked with other journalists who cover the issue, and was interviewed by *Dateline* for "A Pattern of Suspicion."

A New Way of Reporting

Computer-assisted reporting has grown and thrived during the past two decades. It has widened citizens' knowledge of their communities and offered a meaningful way for journalists and the public to work together.

CAR, sometimes called precision journalism, involves the use of social research methods and data analysis to give greater context and depth to news stories and to organize the results of reporting on Web sites so that the readers and viewers can probe more deeply into the findings. Journalists who use CAR work with compilations of public records in electronic form and use common computer programs to discover new information.

As a consequence, the public has reaped the benefits of knowing what kinds of databases the government and business keep and how those databases are used or misused to affect each citizen's life. But more important, journalists and the public can now analyze the databases themselves for public safety, to make government and business more accountable for their actions, and, finally, to contribute to a better and more open democracy.

With databases, journalists have moved from reporting on anecdotal events to revealing perilous patterns and trends. Among the many topics covered have been:

- Unsafe bridges, dams, and railroad crossings
- Home-care nursing care aides with criminal backgrounds
- Dangerous military and commercial aircraft
- Wasteful government contracts
- Fraudulent or flawed elections
- Housing scams and poor bank lending practices
- Failing schools and questionable teaching staffs

These stories go past simply reporting the weaknesses in government and business. They show how systems are failing and how they can be repaired. The journalists often offer solutions. Because the stories frequently are based on tens of thousands of public records, they are far more convincing and credible than journalism that involves only a sampling of records or anecdotal evidence.

In this new approach, journalists have had to learn to use new software tools to find information lurking inside columns and rows of data. For instance, journalists have learned to use the spreadsheet, long the tool of financial analysts, to dissect public budgets and make comparisons among numbers. Journalists have learned how to use database managers to uncover hidden information. Looking for spatial patterns, some have even learned how to map the data and analyze it geographically. Yet others have picked up statistical programs to look for relationships, as a social scientist would.

Many journalists using CAR also have mastered the fine print of open-records laws as they attempt to get electronic information from local, state, and federal officials. In some cases, the journalists and their media organizations have had to wage expensive battles for access to the data.

As many U.S. news organizations trim costs, they have continued to invest in computer-assisted reporting. CAR boot camps in Columbia, Missouri, run by Investigative Reporters and Editors, Inc., and the National Institute for Computer-Assisted Reporting, a joint program of IRE and the Missouri School of Journalism, consistently fill to capacity. Hundreds of newsrooms, print and broadcast, now have at least one journalist trained in CAR. To understand more clearly the results and benefits of these methods, we will look at three topics that matter deeply to readers and viewers: elections, crime, and racial inequality. Additionally, we will examine how journalists have used computer-assisted reporting to bolster public service journalism that seeks to connect readers and viewers more closely to their communities or explain some element of public life.

Revealing Flaws in Elections

The utility of computer-assisted reporting came to the fore in the news coverage of the latest presidential election. Three days after the *Sarasota Herald-Tribune* in July 2004 uncovered a major flaw in Florida's system for purging felons from the state's voter rolls, Secretary of State Glenda Hood reversed course and announced the system would be scrapped. Specifically, the newspaper had reported that a "quirk" in the state's system for identifying felons—who could be barred from voting—had failed to find thousands who were Hispanic.

Two reporters at the newspaper had obtained the state's computerized list of forty-eight thousand felons who would be barred from voting. They then examined the list with a computer spreadsheet program. They were able to see that Hispanics, who make up 17 percent of the state's population, constituted less than one-fifth of 1 percent of names on the purge list. Something was clearly wrong.

The stakes were high for the election. Florida's vote narrowly decided the 2000 presidential election in favor of George W. Bush. Bush beat Vice President Al Gore by 537 votes in Florida after an extended recount and won just enough electoral votes to eke out victory. Cubans make up nearly one of every three Hispanics in Florida, according to 2000 Census data, and tend to support Republicans. So any omission of Hispanics from the purge list could tip the balance to GOP candidates, the newspaper reported.

"Thousands of felons could get to vote this November for one reason: They're Hispanic," staff writers Chris Davis and Matthew Doig wrote in their front-page story. ". . . A data quirk in the state's controversial effort to purge convicted felons from the voter rolls appears to have excluded Hispanics in greater numbers than other races. The missing Hispanics could feed into the Democratic Party's contention that the purge is Jeb Bush's plan to help his brother win Florida in the November presidential election." When the state scrapped the system, officials said that Hispanic felons could have been missed inadvertently because of inconsistencies in the way their race and ethnicity is reported in public databases.

Voting rights advocates in Florida hailed the reporting as a public service that had a real effect.

"Their research showed that the felon purge list was riddled with inaccuracies," said Howard Simon, executive director for the American Civil Liberties Union of Florida. The state ACLU had been challenging the list on the basis that some eligible voters wrongly had been placed on it. As a result, after the state scrapped the list, those eligible voters were permitted to vote, Simon said.

Floridians had already become skeptical about the integrity of the purged-voter list, Simon said. "The work of Chris and Matt simply proved the point and nailed it home."

Elsewhere during the 2004 campaign, journalists were digging deep into other databases to report on the election. Journalists at the *New York Daily News,* the *Charlotte Observer,* and the *Kansas City Star* found people registered to vote in more than one locale. Others at the Center for Public Integrity and the *Washington Post* revealed the influence of so-called 527 committees, relatively new political nonprofit groups that operated free of federal political spending restraints and poured millions of dollars into the elections on behalf on candidates.

The independent Section 527 groups, named after a portion of the tax code, became major players for the first time because of the prohibition of unlimited contributions to national political organizations or candidates contained in the Bipartisan Campaign Reform Act of 2002. The 527 groups are not covered by the prohibition and spent freely during the 2004 race.

How big a role did they play? No one knew until journalists starting looking into the data.

Aron Pilhofer, while database editor at the Center for Public Integrity, suggested in late 2002 that the center take the first comprehensive look at the organizations. Pilhofer led the center in building a database of more than four hundred thousand records using the 527 group filings, which became the basis for an online report called "Silent Partners: How Political Non-Profits Work the System."

The center reported "that the Democrats and Democratic-leaning organizations made great use of a special type of political committee that can raise unlimited amounts of money to influence elections."

The report made national news and set the stage for news coverage as the presidential race gathered steam. Through the campaign, the center reported on 527 spending, including a late flurry by 527 groups that attacked the Vietnam War record of Senator John F. Kerry, the Democratic party challenger.

The *Washington Post* did its own digging into the 527s database compiled by the center. In "Super Rich Step Into Political Vacuum," *Post* staff writers James V. Grimaldi and Thomas B. Edsall reported how a few millionaires and billionaires poured millions of dollars into the 527 organizations working to elect Kerry. A graphic that ran along with the story clearly showed the network of money and politics.

After the 2004 election, members of Congress took aim at the 527 committees, seeking to close a loophole in the law. Senators Russ Feingold, D-Wisconsin, and John McCain, R-Arizona, the architects of the 2002 campaign finance bill, introduced the 527 Reform Act of 2005 in early February. The bill would force the groups to register with the FEC and limit the amount of money they could receive from individuals or committees.

The coverage in 2004 extended the knowledge on election coverage gathered in 2000. In 2000 the outcome of the presidential election see-sawed in Florida on the issue of ballots that registered no vote for president (undervotes) and ballots that registered more than one vote for a presidential candidate (overvotes). Voters watched as Bush and Vice President Al Gore, his Democratic challenger, battled for victory after the polls closed November 7. Mounting court and election-board challenges, political operatives for both candidates worked around the state. Black voters, many of them newly registered by the NAACP Voter Empowerment Program, claimed foul. They said their ballots had been rejected disproportionately.

Dan Keating, a database editor at the *Washington Post* who had reported for a Florida newspaper, looked into the claim. He obtained voter registration data and results from the elections and analyzed it with a computer mapping program. He found that areas in Duval and Miami-Dade counties with a majority of black voters had high ballot-rejection rates. The story confirmed the claims of the black voters and led to further coverage on CNN's *Burden of Proof* and ABC's *Nightline.*

The Florida election battle ended in December when the U.S. Supreme Court halted Florida's manual tabulation of uncounted ballots, thus preserving Bush's slim lead.

With the state bowing out of the recount, news organizations filled the void and produced the public record themselves. *USA TODAY,* the *Miami Herald,* and Knight Ridder Newspapers, then the *Herald's* corporate owner, commissioned BDO Seidman, a national accounting firm, to review the sixty-one thousand undervotes. *USA TODAY,* the *Herald,* and five other . Florida newspapers conducted a separate view of the overvotes.

Bush would have won using two of the stricter ballot review standards, the newspapers reported. Gore would have won under the two more lenient standards. *USA TODAY* posted the data on its Web site for anyone who wanted to look at the raw data themselves, a trend toward transparency in journalism driven in part by computer-assisted reporting.

Another group of news organizations—including the *Washington Post* and the *New York Times*—hired the National Opinion Research Center at the University of Chicago to perform a similar review. That effort also found that Bush would have most likely won if Florida had completed its recount. Members of the public who want to work with the data that the *Post, Times,* and other news organizations used in their reporting can download the data from the NORC Web site at http://www.norc.uchicago.edu/fl.

The intense focus by these computer-assisted reporters on the voting problems that emerged during the 2000 election in Florida exposed the fragility of the U.S. voting system and helped to shape electoral reform.

A History of Improving the Understanding of Elections

In the twenty-first century, political coverage continues to be a staple of daily news. Pick up a local newspaper or tune into a network or cable television news broadcast, and you'll no doubt see a number of stories about political candidates, their words, and their actions. Along with the news comes plenty of spin from political commentators or operatives who work with the candidates. Oftentimes the coverage neatly follows the "he said-she said" model of news reporting: one person's view is reported, then another's opposing view.

Many television and radio political talk shows raise the stakes. By pitting commentators with polarized political views against each other, these shows generate plenty of noise, but rarely shine a light deep into the inner workings of the U.S. political system.

Today, more than 125 years after the demise of New York's "Boss" Tweed, journalists are still keeping tabs on abuses in the political process and uncovering areas where the potential for abuse exists. Increasingly, they are doing it with the assistance of computers.

The concept of computer-assisted reporting actually got its start as a part of election coverage. In 1952, CBS had experts analyze data on a mainframe with the hope of predicting the outcome of the Dwight Eisenhower–Adlai Stevenson presidential race. CBS tried again to project the outcome using computers in 1960 for the John F. Kennedy–Richard M. Nixon match. The experts correctly predicted the outcome, but CBS was too nervous about the new method to release the findings until after the election.

In the late 1980s, before personal computers put number-crunching power on the desktop in most newsrooms, many journalists used index cards to organize, sort, and correlate campaign and election information. By the late 1980s and early 1990s, they began using those personal computers, which sorted more data and did it faster. For example, the *St. Louis Post-Dispatch* in 1990 used computer databases to discover 270 dead people registered to vote in East St. Louis, a city on the Illinois side of the Mississippi River. For more than a decade, journalists and public officials had heard tales of voter fraud in the city. The story by staff writers Tim Novak and George Landau, who did the data analysis, began:

> A man named Admiral Wherry, an Army veteran who owned a barbecue pit and tire repair shop in East St. Louis, died more than two years ago.
>
> But that didn't stop him from voting in the Illinois Democratic primary on March 20.
>
> Wherry was one of at least five dead people in East St. Louis whose names were on the list of voters casting ballots in that Democratic primary, the *Post-Dispatch* found. The five are among at least 27 dead peo-

ple who have voted posthumously in 17 of the past 26 elections there since 1981.

The *Post-Dispatch* also sampled five of the city's voting precincts and found 113 people whose voting addresses were vacant lots or abandoned buildings. Landau, the newspaper's CAR specialist at the time, obtained a magnetic tape with property parcel information from the county assessor. Then the newspaper entered the addresses of voters from five sample precincts into a data table and matched that list with the properties whose value was less than two hundred dollars. The reporters visited the properties to confirm that they were vacant or abandoned.

Unable to obtain Illinois death certificate data, Landau obtained Missouri's data and used the computer to find residents of East St. Louis who died in Missouri hospitals. He used the computer to alphabetize the list. He then manually compared the list of one thousand deceased residents to the East St. Louis voter registration list—a task that took only a few hours.

As a result of the newspaper's revelations, the city purged dead voters from its rolls, and the state of Illinois later agreed to loan ten thousand dollars to help cover the cost of verifying the accuracy of the voting rolls.

In the mid-nineties, journalists began routinely examining the inner workings of the political finance system with data analysis and informing the public of access and influence to elected leaders that had not been quantified before.

In 1996, the Center for Public Integrity, the same nonprofit independent journalism center in Washington, D.C., that built the database on 527s, detailed the overnight White House stays of Democratic party contributors in a report called "Fat Cat Hotel." The center, founded by former CBS *60 Minutes* producer Charles Lewis, obtained a list of the guests and entered their names into Federal Election Commission campaign contribution databases to tally their contributions. In addition, journalists at the center included contributions from the guests' families, companies, and company employees.

The findings: More than seventy-five party supporters and fund-raisers had spent the night at the White House, primarily in the Lincoln or Queen's bedrooms as guests of the president and First Lady Hillary Clinton. Later, in 2000, the center reported that George Bush had gotten $2.2 million from guests who stayed overnight in the Texas Governor's Mansion.

These are just a few examples of ways in which journalists using computer-assisted reporting have deciphered and made clear how politics and elections really work in America.

Crime Solvers

In recent years, journalists at many newspapers and a growing number of television newsrooms have scoured databases to examine police conduct and practices and how they have affected public safety. In the late 1990s, a team of reporters at the *Philadelphia Inquirer* used regular reporting and data analysis to reveal that police had been downgrading and obscuring serious violent crimes in the city's neighborhoods.

It took two years for the *Inquirer* to get the crime incident data. The city police department denied the newspaper's request for the data. The newspaper prevailed when Mayor Edward G. Rendell overruled the police department and ordered the data released in 1997. Then the newspaper found another roadblock.

The police department had removed crime victims' names and police officers' identification numbers from the records. The department also rounded off street address numbers. All of those changes to the data made it more difficult for journalists at the *Inquirer* to match victims in the data with names in police reports.

The team of reporters not only exposed the practice but also shared the city's crime database with the public through the Internet. Citizens could look up crimes online by addresses. As a result, citizens informed the reporters of more missing or understated crimes. From the new information, the newspaper produced more stories that more deeply revealed how badly served Philadelphians were by police who intended to make their crime-fighting statistics look better by misreporting them. And from there, review and reform emerged that led to better crime data and better policing.

More recently, Jill Leovy and Doug Smith of the *Los Angeles Times* used city police and coroner data from 1988 to 2002 to report that neighborhoods in the southern part of the city had twenty-four hundred unsolved murders. They found that police in other parts of the city had solved far more murder cases. Like the *Inquirer,* the newspaper included a database of unsolved murders that could be searched by zip code or proximity to local elementary schools. The *Times* used software to map every single murder and placed the map on its Web site so that citizens could identify where the murders took place in the neighborhoods.

In another example of data mapping for the public, Jeremy Finley of WSMV-Nashville compared prison parolee data to zip codes in the Nashville area. He uncovered an unusual number of felons living in the same areas and trapping citizens in certain zip codes in a "cycle of violence." The TV station provided a list of felons by zip code on its Web site.

In two major inquiries at the *Washington Post,* teams of reporters and editors examined the practices of police when they fired their weapons. The teams examined police shootings of citizens (and police themselves) in Washington, D.C., and a nearby county in Maryland. During the inquiry into shootings by the District of Columbia police, Jo Craven had to persist to get access to FBI data on justifiable homicide by police officers. At the outset, the FBI would not definitely say whether it had the data, so Craven filed a federal Freedom of Information Act request for it. The FBI sent Craven some data, minus information about the justifiable homicides.

When she contacted the FBI again, her contact suggested that she had not asked for the justifiable homicides. So Craven, who had saved a copy of her FOIA request, countered that she had indeed asked for that information. Finally, the FBI provided the data.

Craven also had to persist in her attempts to get data from city police departments across the United States. She filed written requests for data and followed up with telephone calls to the departments. Sometimes she worked her way up the police department chain of command by contacting chiefs or other high-ranking officers.

Eventually, she received data from all the agencies.

On another reporting front, Craven and reporter Jeff Leen had asked the District of Columbia Police Department for a log of police service weapon discharges. The department at first denied that it had a log, but then the *Post* reporters discovered that it was mentioned in a civil suit filed by the survivors of a young man killed by the district police. The lawyer shared a paper copy of the log, and the *Post* used it to write a more targeted request for the database, which the police then provided.

The *Post* stories disclosed poor training and questionable practices that endangered citizens. Those stories led to improvements in training.

Among other newspapers reviewing police shootings, *Houston Chronicle* reporters Rhoma Khanna and Lise Olsen analyzed a database of police shootings and found in their community that more than a third of the shootings were of unarmed people—a pattern that experts said was clearly preventable.

On another topic of concern to the public, many news organizations have recently used geographic analyses to focus on the lack of supervision of where sexual offenders live. Reporter Robin Erb of the *Blade* in Toledo used Ohio's sexual offender registry database and mapping software to show that 25 percent of the sexual offenders in one county were living near schools—a violation of state law. The *Blade* also found that the legislators had not given sheriffs' departments the power to enforce the rule. In other communities such as Seattle, news organizations used databases to show that many sexual offenders were living near day-care centers.

Journalists also have used data about crime to shed light on another subject of public interest: racial disparities in traffic stops.

Investigating Discrimination

Those allegations that the police targeted black motorists at greater rates than white drivers, thus violating the Fourteenth Amendment's equal protection clause, gained credence through the late 1990s as news organizations scrutinized police data. Time after time, journalists from Boston to Seattle found that their local police had stopped, searched, or ticketed blacks disproportionately when compared to whites.

Then in April 2001, Cincinnati police killed Timothy Thomas, an unarmed black teen who had fourteen outstanding warrants. Cincinnati erupted into a week of riots as protesters challenged the police on city streets and set storefronts ablaze. The city's unrest attracted national attention. Andy Lehren, a producer for *Dateline NBC* assigned to look into the shooting, soon found himself asking a question that would lead to a bigger, more revealing national story about the scope of racial profiling: How could a nineteen-year-old amass so many warrants?

Before journalists started using computers and databases in their reporting, allegations of racial profiling went unsupported by hard numbers. Journalists could find black drivers with credible accounts of being wrongly stopped or arrested by the police, but they lacked the means to take a comprehensive look at all the stops or arrests to uncover convincing patterns that would support the anecdotes.

Journalists in 1988 started using computer-assisted reporting to begin examining the chasms that separate blacks and whites in economics, health care, education, and criminal justice. That's when the *Atlanta Journal-Constitution,* in a groundbreaking series of news stories, showed how middle-income blacks had a much more difficult time obtaining home loans than middle-income whites.

Reporter Bill Dedman, with the assistance of university researchers, analyzed Home Mortgage Disclosure Act data that the newspaper obtained from the Federal Financial Institutions Examiners Council under the Freedom of Information Act. The HMDA data at that time included information about every mortgage loan application submitted to banks, savings and loan associations, and large credit unions. The public version of the data provided scant detail about applicants, but it did include information about the location—census tract—of the home that was the subject of the application. The *Journal-Constitution* combined the loan data with census tract demographic and income data provided by a regional planning agency. The story, whose analysis of lending data was supervised by assistant managing editor Dwight Morris, a database and statistics expert, put hard numbers to the complaints of the black community:

> Whites receive five times as many home loans from Atlanta's banks and savings and loans as blacks of the same income—and that gap has been widening each year, an *Atlanta Journal-Constitution* study of $6.2 billion in lending shows.
>
> Race—not home value or household income—consistently determines the lending patterns of metro Atlanta's largest financial institutions, according to the study, which examined six years of lender reports to the federal government.

The *Journal Constitution*'s analysis also found that banks and savings and loans neglected black neighborhoods by closing or failing to open branch offices there. One bank chairman quoted in the story that kicked off the four-day series called the newspaper's findings "damning" and "mindboggling."

Less than a month after the stories ran, the U.S. Justice Department said that it was looking into the lending practices to determine whether any of the lenders were violating the Fair Housing Act or the Equal Credit Opportunity Act. Some of the lenders also responded to the scrutiny by allocating $65 million in low-interest home purchase and improvement loans. The series won the Pulitzer Prize for investigative reporting in 1989 and attracted attention among journalists and lenders. Regulators increased their oversight of the mortgage finance industry, and Congress changed the Home Mortgage Disclosure Act. The changes required all lenders to report the race, gender, and income of all home loan applicants and what action they took on the application.

Other journalists replicated the analysis in other cities using the new data, which provides much more detail, and found similar disparities. Journalists in Kansas City, Long Island, Portland, Oregon, and northern New Jersey reported that lenders rejected applications from blacks disproportionately, compared to applications from whites.

Meanwhile, reporters began looking at racial disparities in other areas of public life. With the explosion of data on school and school district test performance, journalists have been able to determine whether black students are at a disadvantage to white students. For instance, the *Philadelphia Inquirer* analyzed data made available through the No Child Left Behind Act and learned that suburban schools in Pennsylvania had a wider achievement gap between the races than did the Philadelphia inner-city schools. In Illinois, the *Chicago Tribune* found that black students were forty times more likely than white children to attend one of the state's worst schools.

In Virginia, South Carolina, and Texas, journalists analyzed state education data and found that minority students or schools with predominantly minority students were more likely to have inexperienced or unqualified teachers.

Other important issues, too, are now scrutinized by reporters using computers to analyze masses of data. In health care, journalists at *Newsday* on Long Island and the *Plain Dealer* in Cleveland have reported a health-care gap between blacks and whites, and the sometimes deadly implications.

In 1998, the *Plain Dealer* reported: "Black Americans die much more frequently than whites from treatable illness, and the gap in death rates between the races has widened over the last decade." Later that year, *Newsday* reported in its series, "The Health Divide": "Decades after legal segregation ended, blacks and whites in America are largely treated under two medical systems—not separate, but still unequal. . . . The consequences are stark: African-Americans are less likely to get the high-tech, advanced medical care that can mean the difference between life and death, a *Newsday* computer analysis has found."

Journalists have also uncovered disparities in our economic system. The *State* newspaper in Columbia, South Carolina, used U.S. Census data to find that South Carolina blacks hold a disproportionate number of low-paying jobs. Another story by the newspaper found that the South Carolina judiciary was among the least diverse in the country. In neighboring North Carolina, the *News & Record* in Greensboro found that white men controlled the boards of the state's fifty biggest public companies.

Some of the most pronounced disparities came when journalists examined law enforcement and the criminal justice system. Journalists at the *Hartford Courant* examined 150,000 computerized records of bail in Connecticut and reported that judges set bail twice as high for blacks and Hispanics as for whites charged with similar crimes.

More recently, the *Pittsburgh Tribune-Review* created its own database of jury information and mapped juror lists to show its readers how juries in Allegheny County lacked adequate representation by blacks.

The "driving-while-black" flare-up focused journalists on examining police traffic stops, searches, and arrests. The *Boston Globe* found that white drivers stopped by police across the state were more likely than Hispanics or blacks to get released with a warning. In a similar vein, the *Providence Journal* just across the state line in Rhode Island found that "practically every police force in the state searched black and Hispanic vehicles more often than those driven by whites." The *Seattle Times* had reached a similar conclusion several months earlier after it analyzed data from Washington state trooper traffic stops.

With evidence of profiling mounting across the country, *Dateline* stepped in and decided to focus on traffic tickets.

Lehren, a producer for the program, compiled a database containing computerized records of more than four million traffic stops and tickets in more than a dozen cities across the United States, including Cincinnati, St. Louis, Denver, San Diego, and Richmond, Virginia.

For the cities that included a street address for the location of the violation, Lehren used a mapping program to create a point map. He mapped more than one million addresses in six cities. That allowed *Dateline* to challenge police assertions that ticketing disparities happened because the police patrolled heavily in high-crime neighborhoods that tended to be black. *Dateline*'s own mapping analysis showed that the disparity was present in predominantly white areas that had low crime.

Lehren also used a statistics program to calculate ratios that showed on a bigger scale what local journalists were finding in their own cities: Blacks were at least three times as likely as whites to receive citations for driving without a license or for not wearing a seatbelt. During the reporting Lehren and colleague Jason Samuels kept checking their results and running them past experts such as Harris, the law professor at the University of Toledo.

"They did the most thorough and complete job ever by anybody" in the news media, Harris said. "They added depth that I had never before seen."

The hour-long special report, "A Pattern of Suspicion," showed through the story of Timothy Thomas, the teen killed by the police in Cincinnati, how police dealt differently with blacks and whites.

"*Dateline* obtained traffic records that show beginning in February of 2000, as Timothy Thomas drove his friend's car, Cincinnati police began pulling him over, and ticketing him at an astounding rate," correspondent John Larson reported.

Dateline was able to tell the story with personal accounts and hard numbers to a wide audience, Harris said.

"The importance of the story," Harris said, "is I think we have to remember that television is capable of reaching so many millions of people."

The report won a duPont–Columbia University Broadcast Award in 2005 and was featured on "Without Fear or Favor," a PBS documentary.

CAR as a Part of Civic Journalism

Some computer-assisted reporting connects readers more closely to public life in two primary ways: by explaining how the world works and by helping to bring readers and viewers closer to stories that matter in their lives. Computer analysis of demographic, economic, and health data has helped journalists explain everything from migration to work-time driving patterns. For example, the *San Diego Union Tribune* analyzed tax return data from the Internal Revenue Service and the 2000 Census to show readers how the area had lost population. Staff writers Lori Weisberg and David Washburn wrote:

> San Diego County may have a stunning coastline, incomparable weather and a world-famous zoo, but all that has not been enough to stem the flow of residents leaving the region for fast-growing areas in the West where housing is far cheaper. During the latter half of the 1990s, San Diego County saw 16,000 more people leave than move here from other parts of the country, with many of them electing to settle in Clark or Maricopa counties, homes to Las Vegas and Phoenix, respectively, and neighboring Riverside County.
>
> That's a reversal from the trends of the 1970s and 1980s when an average 38,000 more people a year flocked to San Diego County than left for destinations across the United States, according to local demographers.

Census data has proved to be a trove of useful information for journalists reporting on social institutions such as families, neighborhoods, and households. With the 2000 Census, relatively sophisticated analysis of census data became routine as journalists used mapping programs and database managers to detect demographic shifts. Some news organizations have gone beyond that routine analysis to discover deeper meaning inside the data.

Robert David Sullivan, an editor at *CommonWealth* magazine in Boston, used the census and other data to redraw the political map of Massachusetts into distinct political regions, from Bigger Boston to El Norte, with its large Hispanic immigrant population. Sullivan borrowed the concept from the 1981 book *The Nine Nations of North America,* by Joel Garreau, a writer for the *Washington Post.*

In "Beyond Red and Blue," Sullivan did the same for the United States, identifying ten distinct regions. Not all the regions were contiguous. Parts of New England and the Pacific Northwest—separated by thousands of miles and millions of U.S. residents—got designated as the Upper Coasts region thanks to shared demographic and political traits.

Likewise, the *Oregonian* in Portland mapped multiple databases to find the "Nine States of Oregon" and give readers a richer understanding of their community. It also helped the *Oregonian* to shape its coverage of the state legislature.

Elsewhere, journalists have used data to tell readers about the rising diversity of their communities. For example, the *Statesman Journal* in Salem, Oregon, analyzed marriage-license data for a story about the rising numbers of interracial marriages in the state. Other news organizations have used census and economic data to report on lives of the working poor. Reporters at the *Plain Dealer,* for instance, found poverty bleeding from the city of Cleveland into wealthy suburbs where families with workers struggled to make ends meet. Reporters at the *Seattle Post-Intelligencer* found that three hundred thousand people in the state's most prosperous area lived in poverty, despite having at least one family member at work.

USA TODAY, using survey data compiled by its own journalists, found that the emergency medical system in the United States' fifty largest cities was "fragmented, inconsistent and slow." Robert Davis, a reporter for the newspaper, developed a twenty-four-page survey while he was on leave from the paper on a Kaiser Family Foundation health-care reporting fellowship.

But not all explanatory reporting deals with significant civic issues. Some of it just answers questions that perplex or amuse readers. For example, why does it seem like traffic is getting worse around here on early Friday afternoons?

Matt Waite, a reporter for the *St. Petersburg Times,* asked himself that question. So Waite obtained data from the Florida Department of Transportation with traffic counts from nearly three hundred locations across the state. He analyzed five years' worth of data and found, sure enough, that the traffic volumes on early Friday afternoons were higher than on other workdays. He wrote:

The ending hour of Friday seems to be getting earlier for a lot of workers.

Anyone who's shaved a few hours off the old timecard on a Friday afternoon knows they weren't alone when they did it. Rush hour on a Friday comes much earlier—as early as 3 p.m.—compared to the middle of the week.

More cheaters, cutting out early under the nose of the boss? Probably. An early escape on Friday is nothing new (and getting people to admit to it for the newspaper isn't easy).

Sometimes journalism driven by computer-assisted reporting becomes an integral part of civic discourse, whether or not that was intended.

In January 1999, the *Charlotte Observer* began publishing a series of reports about what the Charlotte-Mecklenburg, North Carolina, public schools would look like if a federal judge decided to end decades of desegregation. Using student assignment, school location, and demographic data, Ted Mellnik, the newspaper's database editor, was able to paint a portrait of the schools as they existed under desegregation and as they would be with students assigned to their closest schools. The analysis showed that, under the neighborhood assignment plan, the schools would be less diverse and inner-city schools more crowded.

The *Observer* continued the analysis after the judge's order ended the desegregation plan. As the school administration proposed school assignment plans, the newspaper produced special sections showing readers the new proposed district lines. Many of the parents who attended the public hearings brought the special sections along as a reference. The *Observer*'s reporting helped inform the civic dialogue as the school district navigated historic change.

Other times, computer-assisted reporting or precision journalism has been made part of civic journalism efforts in which news organizations have specifically set out to engage the public. Here are two examples:

In the late 1990s, the *Asbury Park Press* launched "What Ails Asbury?" a classic civic journalism exercise in which the newspaper set up town meetings to listen to citizens talk about community problems. During the course of the forums and follow-up reporting, the newspaper heard stories about housing speculation in Asbury Park. Speculators bought the properties at a low price and then sold them quickly to a "straw purchaser" at prices many times the initial sale price. Fraudulent appraisals allowed the straw purchasers to obtain mortgages for the properties. Journalists at the *Press* used computer-assisted reporting to analyze property data and show the extent of the fraudulent transactions.

Staff writers William Conroy and Nancy Shields began their stories like this:

> During the past 12 months, one company has been quietly buying dozens of residential properties in this blighted city and reselling them within days—in some cases, the same day—for two to eight times the original sale price.
>
> After years of tumbling property values and urban decay, a spike in the city's real estate market might be seen as a promising sign that Asbury Park is finally coming back.
>
> But something about these deals doesn't add up.

In follow-up reports, journalists found similar transactions involving the same mortgage lender in cities stretching up the East Coast. Soon after the articles ran, federal and New Jersey state law enforcement authorities launched an investigation of the property transactions.

Another civic journalism project that used data analysis was the *Savannah Morning News* series "Aging Matters." The series examined issues near to the hearts of Savannah's older citizens, such as nursing home care and protection from fraud. David Donald, then the precision journalism editor at the newspaper, directed a survey that was analyzed with statistical software. The results provided context to readers of the stories.

"Conducting a survey on attitudes about aging proved to be a real service to the community," said Donald, who is now training director for Investigative Reporters and Editors. "It gave insight to older readers so they could see that their cares and concerns were shared with others, while younger readers got a glimpse of what they may experience someday."

As these examples show, journalists have tapped into the power of computer-assisted reporting techniques during the past twenty years to produce compelling news stories that serve the interests of the public and create a base of knowledge that allows the public to make informed decisions about their lives.

Journalism has moved the merely observational to the analytical, finding ways to keep itself meaningful, credible, and distinct from the opinion and bias so prevalent on television and the Web.

Sources

The content of this chapter comes from news stories that have appeared in print, broadcast, or online and are available in the Investigative Reporters and Editors, Inc., Resource Center at the Missouri School of Journalism. In addition, the authors relied on story questionnaires in the Resource Center, Extra! Extra! on the IRE Web site, and articles that appeared in IRE publications, including the *IRE Journal* and *Uplink*.

"Aging matters." *Savannah Morning News.* Available online at http://www.savannahnow.com/features/aging, 2000.

Cauchon, Dennis. "Newspapers' Recount Show Bush Prevailed in Fla. Vote." *USA TODAY,* April 4, 2001, 1A.

Craven, Jo. E-mail interview, July 2006.

Craven McGinty, Jo. "Home Mortgage Lending: How to Detect Disparities." Investigative Reporters and Editors Beat Book Series: Columbia, Mo., 2000.

Davis, Alex. "Mixed Race Marriage on Rise." *Statesman Journal* (Salem, Ore.), January 3, 2003.

Davis, Chris, and Matthew Doig. "Hispanics Missing from Voter Purge List." *Sarasota Herald-Tribune,* July 7, 2004, 1A.

———. "Purged Voter Problems." *Uplink* 16, no. 5 (September–October 2004): 1.

———. "State Scraps Felon Voter List." *Sarasota Herald-Tribune,* July 11, 2004, 1A.

Davis, Dave. "Medical Advances Leave Blacks Behind." *Cleveland Plain Dealer,* May 21, 1998, 1A.

Davis, Robert. "Many Lives Are Lost across USA because Emergency Services Fail." *USA TODAY,* July 28, 2003, 1A.

———. "Survey Helps Explain Heart Attack Survival." *Uplink* 16, no. 2 (March–April 2004): 1.

Dedman, Bill. "The Color of Money." *Atlanta Journal-Constitution,* reprt., 1988.

Ebrahim, Margaret. "Fat Cat Hotel." *Public I* 2, no. 5 (August 1996): 1.

Fazlollah, Mark, Michael Matza, and Craig R. McCoy. "Downgrading the Offense." *Philadelphia Inquirer,* various dates, 1998.

———, and Clea Benson, "Crimes Uncounted." *Philadelphia Inquirer,* various dates, 1999.

Fessenden, Ford. "A Difference of Life and Death." *Newsday,* November 29, 1998, A4.

Florida Ballots Project, National Opinion Research Center. Available online at http://www.norc.org/fl/index.asp.

Foster, Heath, Paul Nyhan, and Phuong Cat Le. "The Working Poor: Hard Work, Hard Times." *Seattle Post-Intelligencer,* February 9, 2005.

Grimaldi, James V., and Thomas B. Edsall. "Super Rich Step into Political Vacuum." *Washington Post,* October 17, 2004, A1.

Harris, David. Interview, April 2005.

Heller, Nathaniel. "Overnight Guests at Governor's Mansion Add $2.2 Million to Bush Campaign." Center for Public Integrity, March 15, 2000. Available online at http://membership.publicintegrity.org/report.aspx?aid=227&sid=200.

Herzog, David. *Mapping the News: Case Studies in GIS and Journalism.* Redlands, Calif.: ESRI Press, 2003.

"House of Cards." *Asbury Park Press,* reprt., 1997.

Houser, Mark. "Unmasking Murder Myths." *Uplink* 16, no. 6 (November–December 2004): 6.

Houser, Mark. "Analysis Finds Juries Lack Color." *Uplink* 16, no. 6 (November–December 2002): 11.

Houston, Brant. *Computer-Assisted Reporting: A Practical Guide.* 3rd ed. Boston and New York: Bedford/St. Martins, 2004.

———, and Jack Ewing. "Justice Jailed." *Hartford Courant,* June 16, 1991, 1.

Landau, George. "Ghostbusting in East St. Louis." *Uplink* 1 (October 1990): 1.

Landis, Bruce. "Minorities More Likely to Be Searched in Traffic Stops." *Providence Journal,* June 1, 2003. Available online at http://www.projo.com/news/content/projo_20030601_search1.8af5a.html.

Larson, John. "Behind the Death of Timothy Thomas." *Dateline,* April 10, 2004. Available online at http://www.msnbc.msn.com/id/4703574/.

Lehren, Andy. "Mapping, Stats Show Scope of Racial Bias." *Uplink* 17, no. 1 (January–February 2005): 1.

Mapes, Jeff, Alex Pulaski, and Gail Kinsey Hill. "The Nine States of Oregon." *Oregonian,* November 2, 2003.

Mendell, David, and Darnell Little. "Data Shows Woes for Middle-class Blacks." *Uplink* 16, no. 1 (January–February 2004): 1.

Merzer, Martin. "Review Shows Ballots Say Bush." *Miami Herald,* April 4, 2001, 1.

Meyer, Philip. *Precision Journalism: A Reporter's Introduction to Social Science Methods.* 4th ed. Lanham, Md.: Rowman and Littlefield, 2002.

Montgomery, Christopher, Bill Lubinger, and Dave Davis. "Working Hard Doesn't Work for Thousands of NE Ohioans." *Cleveland Plain Dealer,* September 5, 2004.

Novak, Tim, and George Landau. "Dead or Alive: City's Ineligible Voters Number in Thousands." *St. Louis Post Dispatch,* September 9, 1990, 1.

Pew Center for Civic Journalism. James K. Batten Awards. Available online at http://www.pewcenter.org/batten.

Ruz Gutierrez, Pedro. E-mail interview, July 2006.

Sancho, Ion. Interview, April 2005.

"Silent Partners: How Political Non-Profits Work the System." Center for Public Integrity. Available online at http://www.publicintegrity.org/527/default.aspx.

Simon, Howard. Interviews, April 2005 and August 2006.

Sullivan, Robert David. "Beyond Red and Blue." *CommonWealth.* Available online at http://www.massinc.org/commonwealth/new_map_exclusive/beyond_red_blue.html

Sullivan, Robert David. "Mapping a New Look at Presidential Results." *Uplink* 16, no. 2 (March–April 2004): 3.

Sullivan, Robert David. "The Ten States of Politics in Massachusetts." *CommonWealth* (Summer 2002).

Waite, Matthew. "Sneakin' toward the Weekend, Workers Fill Roadways." *St. Petersburg Times,* August 1, 2003.

Weisberg, Lori, and David Washburn. "Comings & Goings." *San Diego Union-Tribune,* August 17, 2003.

Wyly, Elvin K., and Steven R. Holloway. "The New Color of Money: Neighborhood Lending Patterns in Atlanta Revisited." *Housing Facts and Findings* 1, no. 2 (Summer 1999).

Stuart Loory

How to Get the Journalism You Deserve

Changes in technology and in attitude have created a relationship between journalists and their consumers that did not exist in the old days of print and broadcast news. Lately a conversation—sometimes a shouting match—has replaced the monolithic pronouncements from editorial offices. The consumers of journalism today have multiple avenues for requests, suggestions, or complaints. Still, free speech in a democracy demands that citizens speak more effectively and that journalists listen more carefully. Stuart Loory, who holds the Lee Hills Chair at the Missouri School of Journalism and whose career has ranged from the Los Angeles Times *to the* New York Times *to CNN, suggests how you can talk to the press.*

The consumers of news today possess a growing influence on how the news business—radio and television, news magazines and the Internet, as well as daily newspapers—does its job. Journalists feel that influence directly, when their work is scrutinized by bloggers, and indirectly, when citizens complain to an ombudsman or a news council. Within the profession, there are growing movements dedicated to self-improvement and to accountability. However, what is still missing—and still needed—are independent, nonpartisan advocates of readers, viewers, or listeners.

Even without such public watchdogs of the journalistic watchdog, those who report the news are being second-guessed as never before. How much credence should all the new complaints get? Different news organizations decide in different ways. Some publish the e-mail addresses of all of their reporters and editors and encourage the consumers to write directly to the "offending" individual. Some have hired ombudspersons, public editors, or readers' representatives to look closely at complaints and other aspects of

148

how an organization does its job, report regularly to the public, and question their organization's professionals. In three states, news councils have been created. Members of the news business and the public who serve hear complaints and then pass judgment on them. The councils are nongovernmental. News organizations recognize them voluntarily. Three foundations interested in the way the news business operates have announced a joint grant to existing news councils to help establish more of them.

Finally, consumers have a great opportunity to take matters into their own hands by broadcasting their comments or complaints around the globe through online access. Sometimes, these critics get results.

In the winter of 2004–2005, bloggers (call them citizen-journalists, press critics, or just members of the public), working through the Internet, were able to raise objections to a report by CBS's *60 Minutes II* and a statement by Eason Jordan, the chief news executive at CNN, that drove Dan Rather, the longtime CBS anchor and reporter on the story in question, to an early retirement and Jordan out of his job.

Rather had been the reporter on a CBS *60 Minutes II* segment based on documents showing that President Bush had lied about his membership in the Air National Guard as a young man. The documents turned out to be unverifiable. Jordan, who spoke at a meeting of the World Economic Forum in Davos, Switzerland, said he knew of twelve journalists who were killed by gunfire from American combatants in Iraq, implying that the victims had been deliberately targeted. American Congressman Barney Frank (D-Mass.) referred to the deaths as "collateral damage." Jordan took that remark to mean Frank thought they had been killed accidentally and that the military had no responsibility for the killings. The news executive disagreed.

WEF meetings operate under the rule that attendees of a meeting may use information without identifying speakers. In common American journalism parlance, such meetings are "for background only." Despite the rule, Rony Abovitz, thirty-four, of Hollywood, Florida, posted an item on the WEF Web blog reporting that Jordan had claimed the journalists were deliberately targeted because they were gathering information. Little did Abovitz, chief technological officer for Z-KAT, a young firm making minimally invasive equipment for orthopedic and neurological surgery and never before a blogger, know that he had started a firestorm that would consume Jordan and blacken CNN.

Abovitz wrote: "During one of the discussions about the number of journalists killed in the Iraq War, Eason Jordan asserted that he knew of 12 journalists who had not only been killed by US troops in Iraq, but they had in fact been targeted. He repeated the assertion a few times, which seemed to win favor in parts of the audience (the anti-US crowd) and cause great strain on others."

Abovitz went on to describe "the real sh . . . storm" that the repeated remark engendered as believers and nonbelievers (generally anti-American and pro) joined the discussion. In general, he painted a picture of what was going on in the room in a 1,108-word report that would have done any professional journalist proud. And then, switching from reporter to commentator, he called on the two American lawmakers in the room—Frank and Senator Chris Dodd (D-Conn.)—to take steps to get to the bottom of whether American forces really were knowingly targeting journalists.

He concluded with a thought on how the public could use blogging to augment the news business: "As a last note, I think that this article is a good pointer to the future of the news: average people, freely saying what they want, as they saw it, for anyone to see. To me, that is freedom of the press."

Actually, Abovitz had discovered for himself something that has long been lost to the general public. That is that free speech and free press are really one and the same. Short of "shouting fire in a crowded theater" (stimulating a "clear and present danger") news business employees or the public have every right to speak out and say whatever they want. For the public, that includes the right to criticize the news business.

A month later I asked Abovitz whether he was happy with the result of his posting and he answered: "No. In my blog and postings I tried to define the best outcome of what was going on (before Eason resigned). . . . The spinning and hiding out was a bad move by CNN and Eason, and the more aggressive bloggers jumped on it. . . . I was one part of the blog swarm asking for truth, evidence, and engagement—not his head, and not spin. Challenging him was the right thing to do, as was asking tough questions, many of which remain unanswered. . . . What the outcome does show is the power of the blogging world—and how media and others will likely be checked and countered in the future. This technological democratization can be a good thing, but it is just a raw force of nature now."

Not all bloggers are scalp-hunters. Some are professional journalists who have opted out of the mainstream, giving up good jobs to pursue a new form of journalism. One of the most prominent and most popular is Doug McGill, who reported on business and culture for the *New York Times* for ten years and later was London bureau chief for *Bloomberg News.* He now operates two Web sites—one for international news and one for coverage of the news business itself—as well as articles for an e-mail subscription list. I asked him if he thought blogging or other Internet uses would help to create better criticism of newspapers. He replied thoughtfully:

> Yes, I strongly believe that developments in online journalism have the chance to evolve into new forms of journalism that serve the needs of citizens better—at least in certain key ways—than newspapers, TV, and magazines do at present.
>
> While the new "hyperlocal" or community-based online journalism has yet to produce a runaway success story, the early indications are that there is a volcano bubbling (and) that one day pretty soon, these types of sites will offer stiff competition to newspapers.
>
> And they will do this because they both a) offer information in more palatable, interesting, and useful ways to readers than do traditional newspapers, and b) they will evolve business models that allow them to be self-sustaining. I would say that these online community journalist sites are today where blogs were about three years ago—very much in the infancy stage. But they are robust infants indeed.

The World of Bloggers

Abovitz of World Economic Forum fame calls the blogosphere the "raw force of nature." Many of its practitioners see themselves as waging a war to bring down the mainstream media—the "MSM" in the new language of bloggers—or to sharply curtail it. Paul Mirengoff is one of three influential lawyers who have started a blog site called Powerline, which took on Dan Rather after the *60 Minutes II* piece on Bush. Another blogger, Dave Eberhart at NewsMax.com, interviewed Mirenhoff:

> The big issue, as Mirengoff explained, is that the mainstream media has "no real relationship with its audience—they still just want to just tell you how it is. Their attitude will prevent them from getting close to their audience."
>
> Such, however, is not the case with *Powerline,* for example, which has "immediate and direct access to the audience through e-mail."
>
> And, furthermore, the bloggers listen, Mirengoff emphasized.

Yes, bloggers do listen to each other, but that is not an argument for accepting blogging as a replacement for professional journalism. Nor is it a reason to say that blogging will become the new medium of mass communication. Bloggers may claim that the form is growing and that it is surpassing the mainstream media. The mainstream media certainly do have a challenge from the blogosphere: how to make their readers, listeners, and viewers understand their capabilities and their importance. News organizations have several different functions—to present fact, background, analysis, opinion, or color in the time or space allotted for noncommercial material. Too many bloggers meld all of those functions into one presentation that confuses fact and opinion. As the headline on the *NewsMax* item of January 31, 2005, indicated, bloggers are pleased with having an impact. It said, "How the blogs torpedoed Dan Rather."

Many in the public feel that mainstream news organizations treat some of the subjects of their coverage the same way. They believe the contention of the bloggers and other press critics that news organizations have an anti-government, anti-business, or anti-establishment point of view that makes coverage suspect. News consumers have every right to doubt or even distrust their providers just as they have a right to compel home builders, automobile manufacturers, food providers, drug suppliers, doctors, lawyers, or their government to provide them with trustworthy products or services. News organizations have not done nearly as good a job as other consumer-product providers in acknowledging their responsibility. There are various reasons:

• Misunderstanding of their audience
• Concern for their own freedom
• A feeling that they had no responsibility for maintaining contact with customers, that that was more the domain of the sales department of their organizations
• A belief that their employees were so professional that they were generally immune from serious error or unethical practices.

News organizations have learned in recent years that such a sense of omnipotence is not healthy or wise. Intellectual corruption has been exposed as a problem in many ways. Reporters for major news organizations including the *New York Times, USA TODAY, Los Angeles Times,* Associated Press, *New Republic,* CNN, NBC, and CBS have all had problems with plagiarism, fakery, sloppy reporting, or other unethical practices.

Some have reacted with new policies for admission of error and correction. Others have tried to make themselves more responsive to public criticism by reporting on their own organizations with as much candor as they would if reporting on others. In some cases, this self-criticism is done by an ombudsman, who serves as a representative of the public within the organization. With an ombudsman, news consumers questioning accuracy, clarity, or political bias have someone in the organization to whom they may address their complaints or questions, and they are assured of an answer, often an answer that would be shared with the rest of the organization's consumers.

As Jeffrey Dvorkin, former ombudsman for National Public Radio and president of ONO, the international society of ombudsmen, put it on the organization's Web page, the movement is growing:

> We've been around for a while—since the 1960s. Now there are more of us being hired in the U.S. and overseas—hearing from readers and viewers and listeners, writing columns, going on the radio and on TV, being the in-house scold and conscience. But do we do any good? Or are we just (as one critic told me) journalistic chiropractors: lots of adjustments but not a lot of cures. Having an ombudsman won't do any good if the journalism is shoddy. But an ombudsman is a sign of a news organization's commitment to excellence. But we don't replace or excuse poor journalism.

Dvorkin is correct. Ombudsmen do not replace or excuse poor journalism. They only expose or explain it. As desirable as ombudsmen are for news organizations, not every small newspaper or station in the country could afford one. Most organizations still do not recognize their need.

Creating News Councils

Three states have established news councils to study complaints against news organizations and report on their findings. It is a movement that many concerned journalists think could help bring more credibility to the business. In January of 2000, some of the leading journalists in the United States signed an advertisement urging development of news councils. When they were first introduced, news councils were seen as an attempt to control the press by outside interests. But a number of prominent journalists signed an advertisement urging the news business to look carefully at news councils. Those who signed included Hodding Carter, then president of the John and James L. Knight Foundation; Gene Roberts, a former managing editor of the *New York Times,* executive editor of the *Philadelphia Inquirer,* and a professor at the University of Maryland Journalism School; Geneva Overholser, holder of the Curtis Hurley Chair in public affairs journalism at the Missouri School of Journalism, a former syndicated columnist, *Washington Post* ombudsperson, and editor of the *Des Moines Register;*

and Bill Moyers, former publisher of *Newsday* and a renowned television journalist.

"In a time when public disenchantment with the news media grows stronger by the day, news councils offer a way out," the ad began. Later it said: "Journalism should welcome the spread of news councils for their help in maintaining our credibility. Against the power of the press, what other recourse will citizens have except our willingness to be open and accountable?"

The ad urged journalists to look at the Minnesota News Council as an example (http://www.news-council.org/home.html). The Web site reports on many complaints by the public, ranging from an inconsistency on one page of one paper in reporting the name of a teenager involved in a serious automobile accident but not reporting the name of another charged with murder.

News councils need not become an infringement on freedom, as some journalists fear. Journalists should be accountable to their consumers. News councils are, along with other techniques to provide accountability, a legitimate mechanism for ensuring responsiveness to the public. Why legitimate? The three news councils in the United States all have memberships divided between representatives of the news business and representatives of the public. A survey of their Web sites shows that they are careful only to consider complaints of importance and that agreeable solutions to the problems can be reached. The Honolulu Community-Media Council, set up in 1970, is the nation's oldest such organization. It encourages those with complaints about news business operations or policies to try going to the particular news organization to reach settlements. If that cannot be done, then it will consider hearings on the complaints.

In 1978, the *Honolulu Star-Bulletin* brought suit against Mayor Frank Fasi for barring its reporters from press conferences. The council tried to submit a petition as a friend of the court. The judge asked it to draft rules for press conferences, which he adopted for his consent decree ordering the mayor to drop his objections to the paper's reporters.

The council has taken similar cases over the years involving politicians and others who have complaints about news organizations.

The Minnesota News Council since 1971 has issued judgments in 139 cases, about 12 percent of the total submitted. Others have been settled before hearings, while in some cases the complaints lacked focus. The council has no authority to impose punishment, nor does it ask for any. It encourages those with complaints to take them directly to the news organizations first. But once a complaint is made and accepted for hearing, a date will be scheduled and the news organization involved will be asked to answer. Sometimes a news organization will not send a representative to the hearing. Such hearings are held regardless, but without prejudice against the organization, says the council.

The Minnesota council also conducts forums on news business activities, problems, and ethics. In 2004–2005, it held such meetings to discuss news media public opinion polling and coverage of polling in election campaigns, coverage of women's sports issues, and coverage of new stadiums. The council also planned in 2005 to hold a noncomplaint hearing on whether small-town newspapers had to comply with the same standards of quality as large newspapers in big cities. That program shows that the council is interested not only in dealing with complaints brought by those aggrieved by the news business but also with professional problems of a more general nature.

Finally there is the Washington News Council (http://www.wanews council.org/), headquartered in Seattle but covering much of the Pacific Northwest. It was also founded in 1970 and over the years has modeled itself after the Minnesota News Council. In recent years it has received twenty complaints against the news business. Thirteen of them were denied without hearings, four were resolved, and of the three on which hearings were held, complainants were upheld twice and not upheld once.

Like the Minnesota council, the Washington organization has held a series of forums on subjects ranging from coverage on war, terrorism, or school violence to coverage of Fat Tuesday. It has also discussed increasing minority access to the news media. A grant from the Knight Foundation will help create two additional news councils, one in southern California and the other in the New England area.

Like those of the ombudsman movement, the benefits of news councils are great. Anything that makes news organizations more responsive to public needs or complaints is certainly to be desired. Just as those interested in a good news report cannot rely on any single news outlet to provide it, so news organizations cannot rely on any single method of keeping themselves in touch with their consumers.

Ombudspersons represent one possibility. Use of the Internet by citizen-critics and citizen-journalists (part-time or full-time) is another. And news councils are one more.

There are, however, problems with the way news councils are organized in this country and the membership on them.

The councils are generally organized upon the belief that they can be used to fend off litigation against news organizations. As the Washington News Council says on its Web site: "The very idea that people can have a say about media behavior strikes many people as foreign. Some people are intimidated by the authority they feel the media possess. News councils are designed to open up lines of communication between citizens and journalists. *They also provide an alternative to litigation, by giving individuals who feel damaged by a story an opportunity to hold the news outlet accountable without going to court*" (emphasis added).

The serious problem with news councils is the close relationship they maintain between news organizations and the power structure within their communities. Members are chosen from big corporations, nongovernmental or quasi-governmental organizations, academia, the public relations business, and other professions. The news business prides itself on exposing conflicts of interest or even the appearance of conflicts of interest. The Minnesota News Council has a member who is senior vice president of Fleishmann Hilliard International Communications. The Washington News Council has a vice president of Hill and Knowlton Public Relations. Both companies are among the largest in the world and have important national and international affiliations. At a time when the public relations business is under a cloud for the dealings of some firms with the Bush administration, it is particularly inappropriate that they should belong to councils that deal with news business criticism. Similarly, the Honolulu council has one member of its board who is a state senator. That as well could color the decisions of the council.

If this review of blogging, the ombudsman movement, and news councils shows anything, it is that criticism of the news business needs the voices of the general public.

Still, journalism has no shortage of self-criticism or of advocates of self-improvement. The most intense are the Committee of Concerned Journalists in Washington and its sister organization, the Project for Excellence in Journalism. The CCJ's former director, Bill Kovach, a former *New York Times* Washington bureau chief and editor of the *Atlanta Journal-Constitution,* and Tom Rosenstiel, a journalist who has published widely in newspapers and magazines and who directs PEJ, wrote *The Elements of Journalism: What Newspeople Should Know and the Public Should Expect.* The book has been translated into ten languages and is used as a textbook in dozens of journalism schools around the country. The book—and the CCJ—define the nine elements of proper journalism this way:

1. Journalism's first obligation is to the truth.
2. Its first loyalty is to citizens.
3. Its essence is a discipline of verification.
4. Its practitioners must maintain an independence from those they cover.
5. It must serve as an independent monitor of power.
6. It must provide a forum for public criticism and compromise.
7. It must strive to make the significant interesting and relevant.
8. It must keep the news comprehensive and proportional.
9. Its practitioners must be allowed to exercise their personal conscience.

The Kovach-Rosenstiel essentials are basic, and the CCJ has begun a campaign to instill them not only in news business professionals but also in the public. At the CCJ Web site (http://www.journalism.org/default .asp) there is a box of tools for citizens, print journalists, TV-radio journalists, online journalists, managers, students, and teachers. On this site, you can find suggestions on how to deal with a news organization—print or electronic.

The two organizations are also planning workshops designed to educate the public on what the news business is and how it operates. It describes the activity this way:

"[The] Committee has developed a program to work with people to identify what they want from the news and to work in conjunction with news organizations and people in their communities about how to get it. These sessions are designed to be constructive public workshops and move beyond public gripe sessions. The workshops are built around creating a common language and sense of purpose between journalists and community members and focus on the concrete rather than the theoretical."

The Kovach-Rosenstiel book is a primer on cementing good relationships between the public and the news business. The CCJ is an important organization, but it could be complemented by another—a citizen's watchdog group founded by organizers who are neither news business employees nor members of special interest groups connected with policy makers, large corporations, professional societies, labor unions, or others who have regular dealings with the news business.

This watchdog doesn't yet exist. It should—there is a need for an organization of true news consumers whose interest is in getting the best output they can but without any news business connection. Such an organization would complement CCJ, not seek to replace it. It would borrow from the CCJ output but its local chapters would also seek to work with local news organization in learning not only the CCJ essentials but also more specifically how news organizations really work. The news organizations would provide training sessions on such matters as:

- What they consider news and what not.
- How they decide what news to cover and what to ignore.
- How they assign reporters to stories.
- Who are reporters and how were they educated and trained?
- How they form opinions if we have an editorial component?
- How they select commentators.
- What is the relationship between advertising and the editorial parts of the organization?

That kind of information would help to educate consumers to make judgments on how the news business does its job. Such a consumers' organization would create and administer an educational program designed to take consumers inside news organizations to learn how the business works and who the people who gather and present the news are. The meetings would be conducted by professional teachers—journalism educators—but would use staff members of the local news organizations as speakers. Tours would be arranged of the facilities—newsroom, composing room, studios, control rooms, computer rooms, as well as the sales, marketing, and public relations offices. The idea would be to make the organizations as open as possible.

Consumers would have to pay for this education. Indeed, the consumers of news would have a stronger foundation for demanding improvements in quality and relevance if they were willing to pay a larger share of the costs of producing that news. Conventional wisdom has it that news consumers are used to paying little or nothing at all to get their news. They are more than willing to let advertisers foot the bill. A typical newspaper reader or cable TV customer contributes 20 percent of the revenue the news business earns through subscriptions, newsstand purchases, or fees. Advertisers pay the rest. If that 80:20 ratio were modified to 60:40 or even 70:30, news suppliers would be alerted to pay more attention to the basic consumers than they do now.

News business managers, noting how circulation drops every time there is a price increase for the daily paper and how newspaper circulation has been declining over the years, think such price increases would drive consumers away rather than attract new ones. But there is also strong evidence that people are willing to pay for information they find useful. Business leaders and investors pay huge amounts for information that can help them in their work. Ordinary citizens are getting used to paying large amounts for cable or satellite television or high-definition television. Unfortunately, not nearly as many consumers would pay more for news as they would for entertainment, but good products well marketed and backed by good service would attract consumers to a news report they valued. The success of the *Wall Street Journal* and the *New York Times* are welcome. They are both truly national newspapers although they have not forgotten their core audiences—New York metropolitan residents in the case of the *Times* and business and financial people in the case of the *WSJ*.

Well-educated consumers would understand the importance of paying for the product as a means of making the news business truly accountable to the public. The news business would have to be educated to pay attention to this kind of group in the same manner that it does to the Green Movement, the anti-tobacco forces, and those on either side of the abortion question.

In the last few years more emphasis has been put on citizen journalism—increased activity by bloggers and other commentators—as a way to influence the news business. The bloggers do represent an alternative to mainstream news that should not be dismissed. But on the other hand they do little to make the mainstream papers and electronic organizations responsive to their huge audience.

A well-reasoned, well-organized, well-financed public movement that could not only stand up to the news business but also offer it constructive criticism and demands would make a difference. The fourth branch of government could also use a check and balance that would be provided by a public group that understands the complexity of the news business and how to best monitor it. Journalists, the watchdogs of our public life, receive a steady barrage of criticism from partisans of the left and right. The watchdogs, and the society they serve, would benefit from the more constructive criticism of news consumers.

Sources

The material in this chapter is drawn from conversations, interviews, publications, and Web sites identified in the chapter, and the author's more than forty years of experience as a print and television journalist. Below are specific citations to guide you to more information. They are also keyed to relevant statements in the text.

The account of Rony Abovitz's blog from the World Economic Forum came from his Web site (www.forumblog.org/blog/2005/01/do_us_troops_ta.html), a telephone conversation, and a February 27, 2005, e-mail from him.

Doug McGill and I had a brief telephone conversation and then he sent me an e-mail on March 1, 2005. He was particularly blunt on the Eason Jordan matter, saying he thought Jordan's resignation from CNN was sparked by his concern that an alleged affair with the wife of slain *Wall Street Journal* reporter Daniel Pearl was what really caused his resignation. All of this is still available at McGill's Web site: http://localman.typepad.com/;/2005/02/eason;jordan;ma.html.

You can access Paul Mirengoff's blog about Dan Rather at http://www.newsmax.com/archives/articles/2005/1/28/172943.shtml.

The following Web sites were all consulted for information about the ombudsman movement in the news business and about the development of news councils:

http://www.newsombudsmen.org/prez.htm for a commentary from Jeffrey Dvorkin.

http://www.mediacouncil.org/history.htm for a discussion of the Honolulu News Council.

http://www.news-council.org for description of the Minnesota News Council's operations. I also had a telephone and e-mail exchange with Katey McCabe of the council staff.

http://www.wanewscouncil.org/ for information about the Washington News Council.

The Committee of Concerned Journalists and the Project for Excellence in Journalism detail their joint program at http://www.journalism.org/who/faq/default.asp, particularly the last question: "Is there a training program for citizens?"

Also consulted was "Four Journalists (Obviously Biased) Talk About Trust and News Councils," *Editor & Publisher* (January 10, 2000): 17.

About the Contributors

Judy Bolch, Harte Chair in Innovation and professor at the Missouri School of Journalism, was for many years a newspaper writer and editor in North Carolina. She helped spearhead many of the changes at the (Raleigh, N.C.) *News & Observer* that put the paper at the forefront of the industry.

She coauthored one of the first textbooks on investigative reporting and has edited two books of columns. Her undergraduate degree is from Winthrop University and her master's degree is from the University of North Carolina at Chapel Hill. Ms. Bolch is writing a book on new ways to generate and develop story ideas.

Glen Cameron has authored more than one hundred books, chapters, articles, and convention papers. He has received numerous national awards for individual research projects as well as the Baskett-Mosse and Pathfinder awards for his entire body of work. Cameron's expert system program, Publics PR Research Software, is widely used as a targeting research tool in marketing and public relations.

He is a coauthor of *Public Relations: Strategies and Tactics,* published by Allyn and Bacon, and he serves on the editorial board of several scholarly journals and book series. Cameron earned a Ph.D. in communication from the University of Texas at Austin in 1989 and joined the Missouri School of Journalism faculty in July 1998.

Sandra Davidson, who holds both a Ph.D. and a law degree, teaches communications law at the Missouri School of Journalism. She is also an adjunct at the School of Law where she teaches media law.

Her writings include "Blood Money: When Media Expose Others to Risk of Bodily Harm," *Hastings Communications and Entertainment Law Journal* 19 (Winter 1997): 225–307, and "Statutory Language for a Model Statute for Access to Government Records," *William & Mary Bill of Rights Journal* 2 (Spring 1993): 29–116. In 1999, Greenwood Publishing Company published the book, *Bleep! Censoring Rock 'n' Rap Music,* which she edited with Betty Houchin Winfield.

David Herzog is an assistant professor at the Missouri School of Journalism, where he teaches computer-assisted reporting and serves as the academic adviser for the National Institute for Computer-Assisted Reporting. He is the managing editor of *Uplink,* NICAR's bimonthly newsletter, and speaks frequently to journalists about computer-assisted and investigative reporting. He has trained hundreds of professional journalists in CAR techniques and is the author of *Mapping the News: Case Studies in GIS and Journalism,* a book about how journalists use computerized mapping in their reporting.

Before his arrival at the Missouri School of Journalism in early 2002, Herzog worked as a newspaper reporter and editor. He served as the CAR specialist for the *Providence Journal*'s investigative team and, earlier, directed the CAR program at the *Morning Call,* in Allentown, Pennsylvania.

Brant Houston is a professor at the Missouri School of Journalism and executive director of Investigative Reporters and Editors (IRE), a professional nonprofit organization of five thousand members in the United States and around the world. He also oversees the National Institute of Computer-Assisted Reporting. Before coming to the school and IRE in 1994, he was an investigative reporter for seventeen years at several newspapers including the *Hartford Courant* and the *Kansas City Star.* He is a coauthor of *The Investigative Reporter's Handbook* and author of *Computer-Assisted Reporting: A Practical Guide.* He also is chair of the Council of National Journalism Organizations, a group of forty nonprofit associations.

George Kennedy is professor emeritus at the Missouri School of Journalism, where he has been on the faculty since 1974. He is a member of Investigative Reporters and Editors and a retired member of the American Society of Newspaper Editors. With Missouri colleagues, he is coauthor of the textbooks *News Reporting and Writing, Telling the Story,* and *Beyond the Inverted Pyramid.*

Kennedy has been a Fulbright Fellow in New Zealand and has lectured in Europe, Africa, and Latin America. He has published in professional and academic journals.

Stuart H. Loory has held the Lee Hills Chair in Free-Press Studies at the Missouri School of Journalism since it was created in 1997. He also edits a magazine, *Global Journalist,* and conducts a weekly radio program of the same name. He came to the University of Missouri from Moscow, his last post in an eighteen-year career with CNN during which he served as Washington managing editor and bureau chief, first correspondent in Moscow, founder and executive producer of the CNN *World Report,* and general director of TV6, the first independent television station in Moscow. TV6 station operated as a joint venture between Turner Broadcasting Company and the Moscow Independent Television Company.

Before joining Turner, Loory worked twenty-eight years in print journalism. He covered the White House for the *Los Angeles Times* from 1967 to 1972, science and medicine for the *New York Times* in 1966, and science, Washington, and the Soviet Union for the *New York Herald Tribune* from 1959 to 1966. He has won several awards and has written three books: *The Secret Search for Peace in Vietnam* with David Kraslow, published in 1968; *Defeated: Inside America's Military Machine,* published in 1973; and *Seven Days That Shook the World: The Collapse of Soviet Communism* in 1991. He has been a fellow at the Woodrow Wilson International Center for Scholars and was first Kiplinger Professor of Public Affairs Reporting at Ohio State University. He graduated from Cornell University in 1954 and the Columbia University Graduate School of Journalism with honors in 1958.

Daryl Moen, a professor at the Missouri School of Journalism, has been editor of three daily newspapers. He is author or coauthor of four journalism textbooks on subjects ranging from reporting to design.

Including appearances at the National Writers Workshops and the Society of News Design annual workshops, he has led seminars for journalists in more than thirty states. He has been a judge in the Society of News Design international competition twice. In eleven countries ranging from China to Lithuania, he has taught professional journalists everything from design to newsroom management. He has redesigned eighteen newspapers.

Geneva Overholser holds the Curtis B. Hurley Chair in Public Affairs Reporting for the Missouri School of Journalism, in its Washington, D.C., bureau. She was editor of the *Des Moines Register* from 1988 to 1995. She has also been a syndicated columnist for the *Washington Post* Writers Group, an editorial board member of the *New York Times,* ombudsman of the *Washington Post,* editorial writer and deputy editorial page editor of the *Des Moines Register,* and a reporter for the *Colorado Springs Sun.*

The National Press Foundation named Overholser "Editor of the Year" and *American Journalism Review* named her "Best in the Business." Under her leadership, the *Register* won the 1990 Pulitzer Prize Gold Medal for Public Service. She has been named a fellow of the Society of Professional

Journalists, and a fellow of the American Academy of Arts and Sciences. She was for nine years a member of the Pulitzer Prize Board, the final year as chair.

Wesley Pippert is one of a handful of print reporters in the United States who have had extended assignments covering state capitals, Congress, the White House, and an international post. He covered three presidential campaigns and the Carter White House, and he was UPI's principal on the Watergate story. His final assignment with UPI was as senior Middle East correspondent, headquartered in Jerusalem.

Pippert is a Phi Beta Kappa graduate of the University of Iowa and holds a master's degree from Wheaton College (Illinois). He was a Congressional Fellow, held year-long fellowships at the University of Michigan and Harvard University's Institute of Politics, and was awarded an honorary doctorate from Gordon College.

Byron Scott came to Missouri in 1986 to take its first endowed chair, the Meredith Chair in Service Journalism, which he relinquished ten years later to concentrate on international journalism. A veteran newspaper reporter and magazine writer and editor in five different American cities, he also has worked as a teacher and journalist in more than forty different countries. He was the school's international programs coordinator from 1994–2001. He previously headed the magazine sequence at the E. W. Scripps School of Journalism at Ohio University.

University of Missouri Curators' Professor **Betty Houchin Winfield,** Ph.D., is a specialist in political communication and mass media history. She is the coeditor of *Bleep! Censoring Rock and Rap Music* with Sandra Davidson (1999) and *The Edward R. Murrow Heritage: A Challenge for the Future* with Lois B. DeFleur, 1986; and author of *FDR and the News Media,* 1994, and two monographs, including "Two Commanders-in-Chief: Free Expression's Most Severe Test," John F. Kennedy School of Government, Shorenstein Center, Harvard University, 1992.

Winfield has also written seven book chapters and ninety-five refereed journal articles, scholarly papers, and encyclopedia articles.

Index